All roads lead to Rome?

The Ecumenical Movement

Michael de Semlyen

Penfold Book & Bible House
P.O. BOX 26, BICESTER
OXON. OX6 8PB, ENGLAND
Tel: 01869 249574
Fax: 01869 244033
E-mail: PenfoldBK@aol.com
FREE CATALOGUE ON REQUEST

Dorchester House Publications

Dorchester House Publications
Dorchester House
Marsham Lane
Gerrards Cross
Bucks SL9 8HA
England

All quotations are from the Authorized Version of the Bible.

Front cover photograph of Pope John Paul II, on 13th May 1991, thanking Our Lady of Fatima for saving his life on the occasion of the tenth anniversary of the assassination attempt.

ISBN 0 9518386 0 1

Typeset by CRB (Drayton) Typesetting Services, Norwich
Printed in England by Clays Ltd, St Ives plc.

Contents

Prologue

'Nobody believed the collapse of Communism would happen this fast or on this timetable,' says a cardinal who is one of the Pope's closest aides. 'But in their first meeting, the Holy Father and President Reagan committed themselves and the institutions of the church and America to such a goal. And from that day, the focus was to bring it about in Poland.'

Step by reluctant step, the Soviets and the Communist government of Poland bowed to the moral, economic and political pressure imposed by the Pope and the President...

The key administration players in Washington were all devout Roman Catholics – CIA chief William Casey, successive National Security Advisers, Richard Allen and Judge William Clark, Secretary of State Alexander Haig, Ambassador at Large Vernon Walters and William Wilson, Reagan's first ambassador to the Vatican. They regarded the US–Vatican relationship as a holy alliance.

The US and the Vatican on Birth Control

In response to concerns of the Vatican, the Reagan Administration agreed to alter its foreign-aid program to comply with the church's teachings on birth control. The State Department reluctantly agreed to an outright ban on the use of any United States aid funds by either countries or international health organisations for the promotion of birth control or abortion.

'American policy was changed as a result of the Vatican not agreeing with our policy,' explains Ambassador Wilson. 'American aid programs around the world did not meet the criteria the Vatican had for family planning.'

(TIME Magazine: February 24, 1992)

The Archbishop of Canterbury Dr Robert Runcie greets
his successor Bishop George Carey at Westminster.
© The Press Association, January 1991

Preface

The author fully realises that aspects of this message are disturbing and controversial and that it will be viewed by some as bigoted. However he particularly asks the reader to stay with him right through to the end, before arriving at a conclusion or assessing the spirit in which it is written.

He wishes to emphasise that his concern is to keep the unity of the Spirit in the bond of peace to bring together believers in Christ, bound together by their common love of truth and their uncompromising obedience to God's Word.

His prayer is that this book might be used to challenge faith and to bring many back to 'the old paths, where is the good way, to walk therein': and, particularly, that Roman Catholics and those in other denominations caught up in tradition, ritual and man-made religion would be enabled to see, as the Apostle Paul and Martin Luther saw, the wonderful simplicity of the Gospel; faith and faith alone, no extras; Christ and only Christ, 'Him only will I serve.'

C.T. Studd, the founder of Worldwide Evangelization for Christ (WEC), who gave away his fortune and abandoned 'the good life' in England, to take the Gospel to China and Africa, expressed his commitment in memorable words; 'If Jesus Christ be God and died for me, then no sacrifice can be too great for me to make for Him.' The martyrs of the Reformation chose that narrow path. They sacrificed their lives, dying terrible deaths to uphold His Word without compromise, and to demonstrate for posterity the simplicity of the Gospel.

There is a need to recover the truth of the Scriptures so that 'we may all be one in Him.' Without love we are 'as sounding brass or a tinkling cymbal;' but love without truth is wayward, lacking Christian virtue.

Introduction

As the history lesson began on a particularly lovely after-noon in the summer of 1953, it is unlikely that many of the fifth form boys attending would have had thoughts for much other than the swimming-pool, the cricket field or other outdoor activities. The topic of the day, the English Refor-mation, did not sound very exciting, and as one of that class, I could scarcely have been less prepared to learn things which were later to totally change my life. Yet what I heard that day captured my imagination and stirred my heart. It did more than that; it enabled me to obtain what seemed to me at the time to be a glimpse of light. Through that one lesson, I felt in a very real sense that I understood what Christianity is and what it involves; sacrifice and self sur-render and an uncompromising love of truth. I was not yet ready, myself, to turn my life over then, far from it; but seeds were planted that day which took root, leading to my conversion to Christ thirty years later.

The History master spoke that summer's afternoon, very movingly, of the martyrs of the Protestant faith and of their stand for truth; as well as of their insistence that the Bible, the Word of God, not the Church, is the ultimate authority for the Christian faith. He described the life of William Tyndale, whose translation of the Scriptures set down the basis for the English Reformation and led to his death by fire in 1536. Light had dawned on the truth, rediscovered by Luther in the Scriptures, that men are saved by grace through faith and not by works; and as the Apostle Paul

9

wrote to the Romans, 'faith comes by hearing, and hearing by the Word of God'. The open Bible that Henry VIII gave to the people in 1538 was the culmination of the work of Tyndale and others, and a wonderful answer to Tyndale's last prayer at the stake at Vilvorde, 'Lord, open the King of England's eyes.'

Once the Reformers had the precious Word of God, they were not about to compromise it. Many of those who died in the fire in England did so because of just four words in the Bible. Had they been willing to set aside these words or at least to give them a 'liberal interpretation,' they could have saved themselves, indeed even been enabled to prosper. They refused to do so. For them, the Word of God was truth and life; and therefore death would have no sting, the grave no victory. The four words from the Apostle Paul's first letter to the Corinthians, relating to the Lord's Supper, were 'in remembrance of me.' In affirming these words they were denying the Roman Catholic doctrine of 'the real presence,' that Christ is truly present in the sacrament, body and blood, under the consecrated forms of bread and wine. They denied transubstantiation, which is at the very centre of Roman Catholic belief, because they were convinced that it undermined totally the finished work of Christ, the once and for all sacrifice of Calvary.

John Rogers, fellow Bible translator with Tyndale during the reign of Henry VIII and father of ten children, was the first of the martyrs put to death under Mary I. He was described by the French Ambassador as being led out to his fiery death at Smithfield in February 1555, 'as if he was walking to his wedding.' John Foxe, the martyrologist, saw him as 'radiant of countenance ... saying the 51st Psalm by the way, all the people wonderfully rejoicing at his constancy; with great praise and thanks to God for the same ... He was burnt to ashes, washing his hands in the flame as he was burning.'

Rogers was given every chance to change his mind. A pardon was actually brought out for him to recant before the faggots were lit. He was asked if he would ' revoke his evil opinion of the Sacrament of the altar.' Like so many others to whom we owe so much, he stood firm. 'That which I have preached I will seal with my blood', he told the sheriff.

Nineteen year old William Hunter refused an edict to attend Mass and receive the Communion because 'it would be sin against God to countenance such idolatries.' His confession was that 'he was in heart and soul a Protestant and dared not in conscience attend the mass.' He was encouraged to persevere in his stand by his parents; 'I am glad my son,' said his mother, 'that God has given me such a child, who can find it in his heart to lose his life for Christ's sake.' Hunter died in the fire at Brentwood in Essex in March 1555.

The burning, back to back at the stake, of Bishops Hugh Latimer and Nicholas Ridley outside Balliol College in 1555 is still well known to many people; as are Latimer's stirring last words which have so inspired Christians over the centuries; 'Be of good comfort, Master Ridley, and play the man; we shall this day, by God's grace, light such a candle in England as I trust shall never be put out.'

'We will remember them,' we say on Remembrance day, as we commemorate the sacrifice of those who gave their lives for their country in the two World Wars. For centuries both church and nation remembered those who lived and died for faith and freedom at the time of the Reformation. We no longer do so. My daughter's illness in St Bartholomew's Hospital, which is located at London's Smithfield, scene of the suffering of so many of the sixteenth century martyrs, brought me to the place of their ordeal. On the mediaeval wall which still separates the hospital from Smithfield Square, there is a plaque in remembrance of the Smithfield martyrs. The wording on the plaque is simple:

'To the memory of John Rogers, John Bradford, John Philpott and other servants of God who a few feet from here suffered death by fire for the faith of Christ. The noble army of martyrs praise Thee.'

It was distressing to discover that the two Anglican churches of today which occupy that very part of the Square, St Bartholomew the Great and St Bartholomew the Less, apparently prefer not to remember. Literature on sale within the two churches tells of the Dominican friars who were living in the cloisters at the time of the fires in the 1550s, but there is no mention anywhere of John Rogers or of other Smithfield martyrs. An officer for both churches dealing with visitors told me that there was no connection between their church and the martyrs; 'They were burned outside; some Irishmen come each year and hold a ceremony there.' This view is reflected in the religious practice of the two churches; in which the sacrifice of the mass is again re-enacted. There is a service of communion, 'in remembrance of me', in the morning, and a rite involving 'the real presence' in the afternoon. Those who died in the fire, ironically at a spot located between the altars of these two Church of England churches, are now forgotten.

The particular significance of that history lesson at Mill Hill School is that at that time, teaching on the Protestant Reformation was given as a matter of course in schools everywhere. Today this is no longer the case. Seen as controversial in an ecumenical climate, such teaching is progressively being dropped. In fact a Department of Education National Working Party recently recommended that the Reformation be left out of the history syllabus of the new Curriculum altogether; although this was over-ruled by the Minister responsible in Margaret Thatcher's Administration.

A primary objective for this book is to demonstrate how important it is for all of us to remember the martyrs of the Christian Gospel and why they sacrificed their lives. At his enthronement at Canterbury in April 1991, George Carey spoke of the example to us of former Archbishops who were martyred. He named the Benedictine monk Alphege and Thomas Becket, both loyal followers of the Pope of Rome. However he did not mention the martyrdom of the first Protestant archbishop Thomas Cranmer, principal author of the major formularies, the Book of Common Prayer and the Thirty Nine Articles of Religion, to both of which the new Archbishop pledged his allegiance at his enthronement. The Roman Catholic Church has canonized Alphege and Thomas Becket.

None of those who died protesting false doctrines, in the fires of the Marian persecution, will be canonized or beatified. They are not 'Saints', especially to be singled out with spiritual merit and treated by posterity as 'holy', and sought after in the spirit realm to intercede in prayer. Indeed the martyrs for the gospel were strenuously opposed to such exaltation of sinful man. They knew that only God is holy. They were simply saints or followers of Jesus Christ, obedient servants of God, whose deeds and example have illuminated the pages of our history. Their courage and obedience to Christ and His Word challenged and broke the hold that religion and the institutionalized Church had on the people. They brought back the simple New Testament message of repentance and forgiveness; personal belief in Jesus and His once and for all sacrifice for sin on the cross, being all that is required for salvation. They knew from Scripture that all comes as a free gift from God, totally undeserved. *'And being made perfect, he became the author of eternal salvation unto all them that obeyed him.'* (Hebrews 5:9). They obeyed Him by believing all of the Bible and living and dying by it and for it.

Such faith is rare today, with compromise everywhere. The Gospel, the light which has illuminated Western civilization, has gone into hiding, as God's truth has been devalued. The leadership of the national Church has spoken of other faiths as 'many pathways to God' and 'many mansions of the same Holy Spirit'. The Commonwealth Day Service attended by Her Majesty the Queen is no longer recognizably Christian, and army chaplains serving the Allied forces sent to defend Saudi Arabia in the Gulf War, disguised themselves as 'Welfare Officers' in order not to offend the indigenous Muslims.

Today in Britain, there is a 'love Gospel' about, which confines itself exclusively to what is called 'the positive'. It is claimed that as long as Jesus Christ is proclaimed as Saviour and Lord, we are all as one in Him. Differences over doctrine must not be allowed to get in the way of this. We can affirm truth, but not confront error. The Protestant martyrs, godly and loving men, could have taken this same position within the wider Church of their day. They could have confined themselves to avoiding all controversy and to agreeing with their persecutors about many of the 'positives'. But, the Scripture commanded them to 'exhort and convince by sound doctrine' and to 'flee from idolatry'. They obeyed; they saw the error and the idolatry, and as responsible leaders, as pastors trusted to guide their flocks into green pastures, they exposed and opposed it all roundly. They could so easily have chosen to look the other way and concentrate on the many truths of the Christian faith which were common ground. They could have elected to please men, rather than please God.

Had they done so, the Church and our country would have remained in the grip of a religious regime centred on superstition and idolatry. Perhaps never in the realm of religious or spiritual conflict, to borrow some of Winston Churchill's famous words, 'has so much been owed by so many to so few.' The danger today is that in opting for a man-made unity based on compromise; and abandoning the Protestant Reformation and the truths of the Scriptures that were sealed in the blood of the martyrs, we are heading back to whence we came.

Foreword

September 1st 1990 was a date of great historical significance. On that day the British Council of Churches gave way to *Churches Together* in Britain, and the Inter-Church Process formally came into being. For the first time the Roman Catholic Church is participating. Indeed it is sure that she is destined to play a major role. *Churches Together in England* (CTE) was launched in St George's Cathedral, symbolizing, according to the journal *The Tablet*, the Roman Catholic Church's 'senior partnership' in the new venture. In a real sense, in the year of the anniversaries of J.H. Newman and Ignatius Loyola's Jesuit Order, the Counter-Reformation, the come-back of Roman Catholicism, was complete. The Protestant Reformation has now effectively been abandoned by the visible Church in Britain and is widely represented as a tragic mistake.

Considering the momentous importance of what had taken place, the September event attracted very little publicity. Few people seem to be aware of the wider implications of this historic happening to the future of both Church and nation. For example, although few see it, Her Majesty the Queen's position as defender of the Protestant faith and Supreme Governor of the established Church is actually called into question and Her Coronation Oath is clearly compromised. Parliament is similarly being manoeuvred into an impossible position, having now missed the best opportunities to determine its constitutional responsibility. The departure from the well-tried roots of our Protestant heritage which is now apparently a 'fait accompli' is deeply dangerous.

On 2nd September 1990, a Sunday, thousands of church congregations stood together in prayer and personal commitment to one another and to the ongoing inter-Church process. All church congregations in all the main denominations in the U.K. were implicated in what took place even if they did not participate directly, unless they had individually opted out. What individuals actually found themselves involved in, other than commitment one to another was not made clear on the day. There was no declaration of belief or statement of doctrine. Fundamental differences have simply been set aside.

All the church groups in membership with the British Evangelical Council (BEC), including the Free Church of Scotland, the Federation of Independent Evangelical Churches (FIEC) and the Evangelical Movement of Wales declined to join, as did many evangelical congregational and Grace Baptist churches. Other smaller denominations that have opted out include the Countess of Huntington's Connection, the Baptist Union of Scotland, the Baptist Union of Wales (English Assembly), the Wesleyan Reform Union and the Presbyterian Church of Ireland.

'We agree to differ,' over the things that matter most, is a fragile form of unity, even when there is such goodwill on all sides. It has been described by concerned evangelicals as 'holding hands in the dark.' For those that love and seek the truth, the amiable pronouncements of Ecumenical leaders and the elaborate compromises of the *Anglican Roman Catholic International Commission (ARCIC)* Agreed Statements cannot conceal the reality; unity has been established on the terms of the Roman Catholic Church. Cardinal Hume, one of the Presidents of the new Council of Churches for Britain and Ireland has not attempted to hide this. In his book *Towards a Civilization of Love*, he has re-affirmed the Second Vatican Council's Document on Ecumenism statement that 'The Catholic Church possesses the wealth of the whole of God's revealed truth and all the means of grace. It is unable to concede a similar status to others'.' Questioned on television about the Decade of Evangelism in February

1991, he repeated that this meant bringing people into the 'one true Church, founded on St Peter, the rock.'

'When Catholics pray for the restoration of full communion with other Christians, they are praying for that unity which the Church believes Christ willed and which is found in all its essential characteristics in the Catholic Church.' ('Faith Alive', 3–37 on Ecumenism, 1988 – as featured in *The Universe*, April 1989).

On 6th January 1991, Epiphany Sunday, *The Decade of Evangelism* was launched at more than 30,000 church services throughout the country. A Novena of Prayer to inaugurate the 'Decade' had commenced with a pilgrimage to the Shrine of Our Lady of Walsingham on 29th December 1990.

Alongside the Decade of Evangelism as part of the Inter-Church Process is the Roman Catholic *Decade of Evangelization* or *Evangelization 2000*, also formally brought into being on the day which celebrates Christ's manifestation to the Gentiles. The original idea and initiative taken for the Decade of Evangelization came from Franciscan Fr Tom Forrest, who now directs Evangelization 2000 in the Vatican, and Irishman, Fr Jim Birmingham. It was based on the vision that more than one half of the world's population will be presented to Jesus as Christians for His 2,000th birthday. This vision was shared and confirmed at Nairobi, Kenya, in 1983 between Larry Christenson, Michael Harper and Tom Forrest.

The Decade of Evangelism was given its European launch at *Acts '86*, when the Anglican Charismatic leader, Michael Harper, sent a message to Pope John Paul II, via Tom Forrest; 'We're with you for a united evangelization of Europe.' Five years later, both Fr Forrest and Canon Harper were at Brighton 91, which followed on from other major ecumenical conferences such as *Berne 90* and *Indianapolis 90*. In May 1989, a group of 100 Pentecostal and Charismatic leaders representing 30 nations had met to pray for the Decade of Evangelism in an upper room in Jerusalem's ecumenical Notre Dame Centre. The vigil was led by Forrest, Harper and Christenson, and those present apparently felt that God was pointing the way for the world conference which took place in Brighton, in England, in July 1991.

The Pope and Dr. Runcie sign the declaration at Canterbury.
© The Press Association, May 1982

Chapter 1

The Background to Ecumenism

In July 1988 the Lambeth Conference of Anglican Bishops world-wide had met at Canterbury and overwhelmingly endorsed the ARCIC Agreed Statements. These statements represent compromise on all the major doctrinal differences between Protestants and Roman Catholics. Earlier they had been steered through the Church of England Synod by George Carey, successor to Robert Runcie as Archbishop of Canterbury and an enthusiastic ecumenist, who has said that 'it is entirely possible that the Anglican Church could disappear to make way for a united world church.' (Interview BBC Radio Three: *Church of England Newspaper*, 3rd May 1991)

After the failure of the attempts at unity such as the Anglo-Methodist scheme of the 1960s, it was felt that a new approach would be required. Instead of simply organising union from the top down, there was a need to place much more emphasis on grass-roots activity among the local churches. Accordingly the British Council of Churches launched 'Not Strangers but Pilgrims' in 1986, with the Lent Course ecumenical programme. This was the beginning of the new Inter-Church Process, which at Swanwick in September 1987 brought in the Church of Rome, which had now progressed in Cardinal Hume's words 'from co-operation to commitment'. The inter-mingling of different traditions at the local level, allied to what Archbishop Runcie described as 'the reformulation of doctrine', as prescribed in the nineteenth century by John Henry Newman, was the clear way forward.

Unity through the compromise of doctrine had become the objective and the near unanimous vote at Lambeth seemed to point towards unity with Rome at almost any price. The Vatican's response of January 1989, which held out for statements of faith even closer to her own and the Pope's cool reception of the eager Archbishop of Canterbury, Robert Runcie, at the Vatican in September 1989, indicate that movement is essentially in one direction.

This momentum towards unity, an enthusiasm among the 'Protestant' denominations verging on abandon, has accelerated dramatically during the last few decades. How has this come about?

Early Moves Towards Unity

The Reformed faith of Anglicans and Free Churchmen had been eroded over the centuries by the Counter-Reformation, and particularly in the nineteenth century, after the 1833 launch of the *Oxford Movement* in the Anglican Church, by John Henry Newman and the other Tractarians. As belief in the Bible was diminished by humanism, rationalism and liberal theology, Roman Catholic tradition was held firm and strengthened by the new Anglo-Catholic group in the Church of England. By the beginning of this century High Anglicans had joined liberal traditionalists in key positions at the head of the church, doctrinal differences were down-graded and ecumenism was well and truly under way.

The aim of the ecumenical movement is to achieve one world communion; to bring all churches, denominations, and ultimately all religions together. Dr Runcie told the Lambeth Conference that he saw ' no difference between the quest for the Church's unity and the quest for the unity of all mankind.' Cardinal Hume spoke in like manner, in October 1990; 'we have to concentrate on what unites us – it's so simple and yet so profound – we have to concentrate on our common humanity.' ('Nostra Aetate', 25th anniversary of declaration; Universe, 4th November 1990)

The ecumenical movement was not to be described as such until much later as Rome began to become involved. The term 'oikoumene', used many times in the New Testament means 'the whole world' , although sometimes it is used to refer to a major political entity, such as the Roman Empire.

The World Missionary Conference at Edinburgh in 1910 brought the beginnings of the Faith and Order movement, which became the modern ecumenical movement. This third Missionary Conference included Anglo-Catholics for the first time and was chaired by American Methodist John Mott, whose watchword in a lifetime of missionary effort was 'the evangelization of the world in our generation.' Edinburgh 1910 and John Mott's prophetic vision lent inspiration to the founding of Christian Unity Week, organised today by the World Council of Churches and the Vatican's Council for Christian Unity, which celebrated its 80th anniversary in 1990. *Edinburgh 1910* also lent inspiration to the staging of *Brighton 91*, according to organiser Michael Harper, especially in expressing the desire to reach out to Roman Catholics and Greek Orthodox and include them in the future. The *Life and Work Conference*, which convened at Stockholm in 1925 and Oxford in 1937, had as its slogan, 'doctrine divides, service unites', will surely find an echo at the great ecumenical gatherings of the 1990s.

Paralleling *Life and Work* in the '20s and '30s was the *World Conference on Faith and Order*, which led to the *World Council of Churches (WCC)* being formed in 1948 to include the Greek Orthodox Church but without the participation of Rome. One of the founding fathers of the WCC and the first president of the *British Council of Churches (BCC)*, in 1943, was William Temple. At the 1937 Edinburgh Conference, Temple, then Archbishop of York and later a much respected Archbishop of Canterbury who had a major role in the formation of the WCC, spoke of 'the sin of divisiveness in Christendom.' Was he condemning the Reformation itself then? Dr Temple, who was earlier Rector of St James, Piccadilly and had long cherished his dream of Church unity, concluded; 'A calmer wisdom is needed and Christians should avoid zealousness to that point which makes us blind to supplemental truths.' The 'supplemental truths' referred to were not defined, but we shall be considering later some of the traditional Roman doctrines that he may have had in mind.

Yet Rome stayed out of the *Faith and Order Movement*. Approaches to the Vatican, including that of Edinburgh 1910, met with a cool reception. Clearly the timing was not yet right. The Evangelical wing within the World Council of Churches still remained powerful, and doctrinal differences were clear and distinct. It must have become evident to those making the running that it would be the WCC, and in Britain, the B.C.C. that would have to bridge the divide. Rome is, and always has been, crystal clear on her stated position regarding matters of doctrine:

> 'There can be no change in any dogma or basic teaching of the Catholic Church, for such a change would be a denial that the Church is the true Church founded by Christ' (Catholic Register 1961).

Rome's motto is 'Semper eadem', (Always the Same), and she sees herself as 'the one true Church'. Unity looked impossible.

Suddenly and remarkably, everything changed. At the beginning of the 1960's a new warmth and co-operation flowed forth from Rome. Marked by the Second Vatican Council[1] and the Papacy of John XXIII, the doors to unity were flung open. Dialogue had been going on behind the scenes. Archbishop of Canterbury, Geoffrey Fisher, had met the Pope in 1960 and a few months later the Queen, sworn to defend the Protestant Faith, was received, attired in black and wearing a veil. There was, however, another factor, a new dimension, in the wider Church that could

---

[1] More correct is to say that the doors of unity were presented as having been thrown open. Every Bishop attending made this declaration at the Council: '...As well as I do condemn and regret and bring anathema to all that is in contradiction with the faith, and all the false doctrines which the Church has condemned and anathematized. This true Catholic Faith out of which no one can be saved, which I freely here confess and to which I am attached, I am decided to confess it constantly and to keep it pure and without mixture till the last breath of my life.' (*Reformation Review*, October 1963, p 35)

account for the change in the attitude of the Roman See; and that factor was the Charismatic Renewal.

Renewal

The Charismatic Renewal movement, which began in the 1950's with so many apparent virtues, had rapidly swept across the Christian world. It was widely seen as capable, with a great outpouring of the Holy Spirit, of transforming the whole church. Englishman, Donald Gee, a leader in the Pentecostal movement and prominent ecumenist, called it 'the new Pentecost.' Key figure in the new ecumenical 'Pentecost' was David du Plessis, who played the leading role in developing Roman Catholic-Pentecostal dialogue. He was an invited guest at Vatican II and attended all six assemblies of the WCC, from Amsterdam (1948) to Vancouver (1963). As *Time* magazine observed;

> 'No one in the twentieth century so effectively linked three of the major movements of the time – the Pentecostal movement, the ecumenical movement, and the charismatic movement,' as did 'Mr Pentecost', David Du Plessis.

This Pentecostal outreach, beyond Pentecostal boundaries, received its first organised expression in the *Full Gospel Businessmen's Fellowship International (FGBMFI)*, which sprang to prominence in the United States at that time. Founded by Demos Shakarian, a Californian millionaire dairy-farmer of Armenian Pentecostal background, the FGBMFI, from its first meeting in 1951, was closely associated with America's leading American healing evangelists including Oral Roberts, William Branham and T.L. Osborn. It was conceived as an organisation of Spirit-filled businessmen to evangelize and witness to non-Pentecostals, without bringing converts into the Pentecostal denomination. Distinctively Pentecostal blessings and phenomena would occur and, as described by the Pentecostal Fellowship of North America; 'the full Gospel, including holiness of heart and life, healing for the body, and baptism in the Holy

Spirit, with the evidence of speaking in other tongues as the Spirit gives the utterance.'

Like other 'para-church' groups which led the charismatic movement in the '50s and '60s, the FGBMFI brought Roman Catholics and Protestants together in the 'unity and love of the Spirit', placing emphasis on experiential testimony rather than on Scripture. Controversy was to be avoided; difficulties that arose over doctrine, discouraged.

In much the same way, at the same time, Billy Graham's crusades were sweeping aside doctrinal differences with the evangelist going out of his way to recognise 'the role in the Christian family of our Catholic brethren.'

Leading proponents of unity such as the Archbishop of Canterbury, Michael Ramsey, described 'the whole ecumenical enterprise as the Holy Spirit working in us, uniting us in love and building us up in the truth.' Problems posed by articles of belief, confessions and creeds were to be put to one side. Rather than search the Scriptures daily, whether those things were so, as the Bereans did in New Testament Macedonia, new converts received encouragement in the Renewal to rely more on emotion and experience. 'We must avoid binding the Spirit by our stupidity and narrowness and lack of faith,' insisted Archbishop Ramsay, who in 1957 had described English evangelicalism as heretical and sectarian. The combination of mass evangelism and the excitement of the Charismatic Renewal had become caught up with and harnessed by the Ecumenical Movement.

The Second Vatican Council

At the Second Vatican Council, the Roman Church, responding to the heady atmosphere and the promise of submergence of old differences, gave its blessing to this new movement of the Holy Spirit. Cardinal Augustin Bea, Jesuit Confessor to Pius XII, key figure behind ageing Pope John XXIII, and destined to do more for the ecumenical movement and the inter-faith synthesis than perhaps anyone else, pointed the way ahead:

'The Church must first strive to revitalise its own inner life, so that it can be manifested to our separated

24

brethren, an ever clearer image of Christianity according to the Gospel.'

It was significant that 'separated brethren' had replaced 'heretic' (and other terms) in the Mother Church's vocabulary. In 1965 the Second Vatican Council had decreed that 'the separated brethren should be welcomed back into the fold.' A demonstration of this was Cardinal Bea's invitation to David du Plessis to attend as his guest at the third session of Vatican II.

Remarkably, the Roman Catholic Church officially adopted its own Renewal movement, the only denomination to do so. Cardinal Leon Joseph Suenens, Primate of Belgium, Archbishop of Malines, and a rising star in the Curia, was soon to be put in charge at the Vatican and the new movement enjoyed the active support of the new President of the Secretariat for promoting Christian Unity, Cardinal Bea, as well as Pope Paul VI and their successors. Fred Ladenius, Director of the FGBMFI's *Voice* magazine, in his book, *Amazing John*, related how the dying Pope John XXIII had prayed for 'a new Pentecost' for the Church of Rome, a prayer many believe was answered in the beginning of the Catholic Charismatic Renewal just five years later, at Duquesne University, Pittsburgh in 1967. (*Amazing John XXIII*: Gift Publications, Costa Mesa, CA, 1980) CCR overseer, Cardinal Suenens, wrote his influential ecumenical book, *A New Pentecost*, in 1975.

In the United States the Catholic Charismatics were the first to hold their own conference, in 1970; the same year that they established their National Service Committee. The International Communications Office (ICO) was established at first at Ann Arbor, Michigan, in 1972, moving in 1976 to Brussels to be in closer contact with Cardinal Suenens, and then in 1981 to Rome, when it changed its name to *International Catholic Charismatic Renewal Office (ICCRO)*, with Fr Tom Forrest as Director. ICCRO is under the direct supervision of the International Council of the Catholic Charismatic Renewal, which was also chaired by Tom Forrest.

Cardinal Suenens, the Roman Catholic Primate of Belgium, addressing a press conference at St. Bride's Church, Fleet Street, London.
© The Press Association, October 1972

The Spirit of Truth

> *'When he, the Spirit of Truth, is come, he will guide you into all truth.'*
> John 16:13

In his 1980 booklet, *Charismatic Crisis*, Anglican Renewal leader, Michael Harper noted that; 'The Charismatic

Renewal does not have a particularly good track record when it comes to concern for the truth. I am chiefly here referring to the truth about Christianity. Because of its emphasis on "testimony" at least in its formative years, it has tended to softpedal, even to ignore truth, largely out of fear that it will divide Christians rather than unite them. Many Christians have in the past been caught up in sectarian battles over words and doctrines, and it has been refreshing to de-fuse much of that animosity and side-track many of the big issues which previously divided Christians, and to find a new unity in one's experience of the Holy Spirit. But such a unity is bound to last only so long as one can survive on "testimony theology"; and that is not for long.'

Great hopes have been vested in the Renewal Movement. Many Protestants believed that Spirit-filled Catholics, exposed to the Scriptures, would bring about change in the Catholic Church; that Biblical truths would reassert themselves, superstition and idolatry diminish, traditions would be discarded, and that Roman Catholicism would be dramatically reformed from within. These are still the expectations of many. Without any evidence at all that renewed Catholics reject their Church's Dogma, Protestant Charismatics assume it to be so. It is true that many ecumenical Catholics do not discuss their deeply held beliefs; but very rarely are they asked to do so. The view that Catholic reform is real is well represented by a letter from a young Catholic who recently wrote to a Christian magazine; 'Although I oppose the totally unChristian institution of the Roman Catholic Church, the fact is that there is a great reformist movement within that preaches the Gospel of Jesus without putting the doctrines of Rome to the fore.'

However when examined closely, this does not seem to be so. Dr Kevin Ranaghan, who chaired the first major ecumenical conference at Kansas City in 1977, and at the New Orleans 1987 Congress of Renewal supervised the statement of policy signed by all speakers (including Kenneth Copeland, James Robison and John Wimber), stressed to that Congress that 'Catholics are not putting aside Catholic convictions.' 'It is also important to note,' he said, 'that the outpouring of the Holy Spirit in these days has occurred to

Catholics within the Catholic Church.' Another renewal leader, Roman Catholic Bert Ghezzi, editor of *Charisma*, a leading 'Protestant' Charismatic magazine in the USA, spoke enthusiastically for his wife and himself; 'Traditional devotions such as those to Mary have become meaningful to us. The sacramental life of the church has become especially more meaningful, particularly the sacrament of penance which we both use now with greater fruit than ever before.' (*Catholic Pentecostalism* by Kevin Ranaghan, 1969)

Fire, a Catholic group committed to evangelism and renewal of the Catholic Church, 'sets out to challenge and strengthen the commitment of faithful Catholics to the sacraments, Mary, the Roman Pope and bishops, as they guide us in matters of faith and morals.' This was the message on the *Fire* (Faith, Intercession, Repentance and Evangelism) brochure distributed at the 1987 New Orleans Conference on the Holy Spirit and World Evangelization.

Tom Forrest, the key figure in charge of Rome's Decade of Evangelization programme and at the head of the whole Catholic Charismatic Renewal organisation, certainly puts the doctrines of Rome to the fore. At a training session for Roman Catholics at Indianapolis '90, he spoke with enthusiasm and deep conviction about his renewed faith. In view of his importance to the ecumenical movement of the 1990s, he is quoted here at some length:

'My job, my role, our role in evangelization is not just to make Christians. Our job is to make people as richly and fully Christian as we can make them by bringing them into the Catholic Church. ... No, you don't just invite someone to be a Christian. You invite them to become Catholics. You invite them to come with you as a new parishioner of your Catholic Church. Why should this be so important? Let me quickly give you a few reasons.

'First of all, there are seven sacraments, and the Catholic Church has all seven. If that's how many Christ instituted, that's how many I want. So as Catholics we don't have only baptism as sacrament of initiation, we also have confirmation, initiating us into full Christian maturity, commissioning us and empowering us as soldiers of Christ just the way Bishop McKinney was saying in the mass.

'We don't just have the Eucharist as a symbol of the body and blood of Christ. On our altars we have the body of Christ; we drink the blood of Christ; Jesus is alive on our altars, as offering and as a banquet of love. It's a love marriage act. We become one with Christ in the Eucharist, the very body of Christ.

'I remember in the parish that Giovanni mentioned in Puerto Rico, opening the doors to the church to a broad parish public sacrament of anointing of the sick. The church was filled. So many people got healed that I was afraid ever to do it again. For months afterward people were coming into the confessional and into the office to tell how they were healed by that sacrament; and it doesn't just heal the sick; it opens the doors of paradise and deals even with the temporal punishment due our sins. What a sacrament! What a church! What a Christ!

'And we can add to this the full deposit of faith, protected and perfected in its expression by 2000 years of tradition. As Catholics we have Mary: and that Mom of ours, Queen of Paradise, is praying for us till she sees us in glory.

'As Catholics we have the papacy, a history of popes from Peter to John Paul II. As Catholics we have the rock upon which Christ did build his church. ... We're ten years short of 2000 years, and our job is to use this remaining decade evangelizing everyone we can into the Catholic Church, into the body of Christ, and into the third millenium of Catholic history.'

In the early days of the Renewal Movement, such forthright and controversial declarations of commitment to Roman Catholic beliefs were not publicly stated by CCR leaders. Charismatic speakers were at pains to avoid all areas of disagreement, relating to faith and practice. Influential Protestant leaders of the 60's and 70's became convinced that the renewal was the road to reform and to unity.

The Evangelical Divide

At the 1977 *National Evangelical Anglican Congress (NEAC)* at Nottingham, David Watson spoke of the Reformation as 'one of the greatest tragedies that ever happened to the church' and went on to tell of when he had attended a Catholic/Protestant charismatic conference in Dublin, 'how he had come to sense the profound grief that God must feel at the separation of his body.' (*Evangelicals Tomorrow*: John Capon, Collins, Glasgow).

Michael Harper, has spoken of his own ecumenical pilgrimage in terms of 'the three major spiritual influences in the contemporary church.' In his book, *This is the Day*, Canon Harper speaks of three sisters whose names are Evangeline, Charisma and Roma, representing the Evangelical and Charismatic movements and the Roman Catholic Church, 'which was once anathema to him, but in which he has found a deepening of his profound, loving commitment to Christ and God.'

Brother Ramon of the Anglican Society of St Francis, writing this in his handbook on spiritual retreats, continues:

> 'When Michael's prejudices had melted ... he came to love those he had previously rejected, meeting Christ in them, and learning from the Holy Spirit through them. The treasure stores of catholic life opened their riches to him. In a disarming biblical manner he says; "The Virgin Mary has come alive and I feel I know her now, in the same way as my evangelical heritage helped me to know Saint Paul." God's creation, gifts of creativity, nature and nature's art all came to life, and the Church corporate, with its pre-Reformation riches, took on a new meaning. The sacraments were no longer lifeless mechanical rites, but effectual signs that work where there is faith. Since meeting Roma, holy communion became an oasis in a parched desert.'
> (Brother Ramon SSF: *Deeper Into God*, pp 81 & 83, Marshall Pickering, 1987)

Leading evangelical John Stott, an advisor to the World Council of Churches, told the Nottingham NEAC Conference that 'the visible unity of all professing Christians should be our goal ... and evangelicals should join others in the Church of England in working towards full communion with the Roman Catholic Church.' That same year, 1977, John Stott went to Venice to be part of the *Evangelical-Roman Catholic Dialogue on Mission*. Respected evangelical theologian J.I. Packer has added his weight to the arguments in support of ecumenical renewal; 'Do I see renewal in the Roman Catholic Church? As a Protestant for whom major elements of official Catholicism represent Christianity skewed, I reply that I do. It is as these ... streams of renewal continue to flow, and hopefully converge, that the Catholic Church will give most to the rest of Christendom and to the benighted pagan world of our time.' (*New Covenant* magazine, February 1988).

American evangelical David W. Cloud takes an entirely different view of what is going on; 'From Rome's perspective there could not be a more effective instrument towards the agenda set forth by Rome, which is building up the Catholic Church and re-establishing Catholic dominion, than the gullible misled Charismatic movement. It is a movement which by claiming to believe that Catholics and all people need to be "born again", sees absolutely no need of warning of Rome's wretched and blasphemous errors or of instructing those who are saved to come out of that apostasy. Rome has found a winner.'

Concerned Protestant groups like the Church of England's *Church Society* and the *Protestant Alliance*, founded by the 7th Earl of Shaftesbury, claim that the price of charismatic renewal and 'neo-evangelicalism' is much too high. Dr David Samuel, the Director of Church Society, writing in 1990, warned that 'we are seeing the revivifying of that ancient regime with its focus in the papacy, something which we might not have believed possible in 1870 when the Pope's temporal power was eclipsed and the fortunes of the Vatican seemed to be declining. We have seen a remarkable revival of that institution, which is intended to head up an ecclesiastical empire created by the ecumenical movement.' (The End of the Ecumenical Movement: The Harrison Trust, 1990)

The Ecumenical Movement has gained considerable, if

A placard demonstration protesting against the Archbishop of Canterbury's trip to Rome to see the Pope. The Rev. David Samuel, director of the Church Society, led the protest.

© The Press Association, September 1989

not irresistible momentum, as Protestant leaders see it. Vital differences in belief have become blurred and the Protestant reformation virtually reversed. George Ashdown, Secretary of the Protestant Alliance, believes that Christians need a clear reminder of these things:

> 'The Reformers saw the whole Catholic system as anti-Christian. Luther and Calvin went so far as to identify the Papacy with the Antichrist and they like Wycliffe, Tyndale, Matthew Henry, Spurgeon, Lloyd-Jones and many others saw the Roman Catholic Institution as Mystery Babylon, the Mother of Harlots, vividly described in Revelation chapter 17.'[2]

---

[2] It is important to note that 'anti' from the Greek in the Bible often means 'substitute' or 'taking the place of'; not necessarily 'against'. 'Vicar of Christ', one of the titles that the Pope takes to himself carries the same meaning as 'antichrist', that is he who takes the place of or stands in for Christ.

Chapter 2

Roman Catholic Doctrine and the Mass

What Archbishop Temple had called 'supplemental truths' had been described, by the Protestant reformers as 'errors' – errors which when confronted led to persecution, the Inquisition, martyrdom and to secession or schism.

'These were among the leading doctrines of the Church of Rome, condemned in plain and unmistakable language nine times over by the 39 Articles of the Church of England,' wrote Bishop J.C. Ryle in 1885.

A further problem for contemporary Protestants is that the 'errors' have been compounded since the 16th century. The principles embodied by the Roman Catholic Church in the Council of Trent (1545), confirming the dogma or error, have been reaffirmed by successive Popes, including John Paul II today. But added to them now are the three new doctrines or 'dogmas' of Papal Infallibility (1870), the Immaculate Conception (1854) and the Assumption into heaven of Mary, 'Mother of God' (1950). Contrary to the understanding of very many people, Vatican II reversed no doctrine of the Church, nor did it make any recommendation to do so.

Salvation

Fundamental to the whole doctrinal divide is the issue of salvation itself. Justification by faith alone, according to Rome, is not sufficient. More grace is needed. This, we are told is obtained through the sacraments; by further works and infused righteousness, leading into the doctrines of penance, purgatory, and plenary indulgences. Baptism, they say, is essential. The Church insists that Roman Catholics must be baptised in order to be saved. The Catechism defines Baptism as the sacrament that gives our souls the new life of sanctifying grace by which we become children of God and heirs of heaven. It is necessary for the salvation of all men because Christ has said: *'Unless a man be born again of water and the spirit, he cannot enter into the kingdom of God.' The Second Vatican Council* confirmed the longstanding dogma of Pope Boniface VIII of 1301, 'Extra Ecclesiam Nulla Salvus' ('no salvation outside of the Church of Rome.'); 'It is through the Catholic Church alone that the whole fullness of the means of salvation can be obtained. All are obliged to belong to the Catholic Church in order to be saved.' (*The New St Joseph Baltimore Catechism*: Catholic Book Publishing, New York 1968)

Luther denied all this strenuously. He described justification by faith without works as 'the article of a standing or falling church,' and he and the other Reformers believed that Rome had unchurched herself and forfeited any right to the loyalty of men by denying the Scriptural way of salvation.

Bill Jackson, who boldly directs a ministry called *Christians Evangelizing Catholics*, in Louisville, Kentucky, speaks today with the same conviction; 'Full forgiveness of sins which are gloriously removed, "as far as the east is from the west", when we are redeemed through the completed work at Calvary, is replaced by priestly absolution, repeated confession, penances and good works. Also a confining and binding sense of guilt stands wholly in conflict with the truth in God's Word concerning the cleansing and liberating of the blood of Christ.'

The great doctrine of grace at the heart of the Gospel is overthrown.

> *'For by grace are ye saved through faith; and that not of yourselves; it is the gift of God: not of works, lest any man should boast.'* Ephesians 2:8, 9

Luther, a formidable theologian equipped with a mighty intellect and prodigious learning, after a lengthy and painful search for God and for assurance of salvation, discovered that he needed to lay all these things down in order to meet his Lord. Like so many millions of other Christians before and since, he came to see the truth regarding the simplicity of the new birth; as Paul told the Romans; *'The just shall live by faith'* and, *'if thou shalt confess with thy mouth the Lord Jesus, and shalt believe in thine heart that God hath raised him from the dead, thou shalt be saved.'* (Romans 1:17 and 10:9)

The Mass

At the heart of Roman Catholicism is the Mass or Eucharist, described by the Second Vatican Council as 'the fount and apex of the whole Christian life.' Kilian McDonnell, a distinguished Catholic theologian and President of the Institute for Ecumenical and Cultural Research, Minnesota, has spoken of how 'many will attest that one of the best expressions of the Renewal is its Eucharist celebrations. In France, for instance, a number of important communities centre their very lives around the Eucharist.'

Mary McCarthy, another Renewal leader, testified that 'attendance at daily Mass has grown to be my way of life. Through the Mass I receive the strength I need to witness to Christ and His teachings.' (K. Ranaghan, op.cit. p 32)

Rome claims that the Mass is a sacrifice. It is held to be 'one and the same Sacrifice with that of the Cross, in as much as Christ, who offered himself, a bleeding victim, on the Cross to his heavenly Father, continues to offer himself in an unbloody manner on the altar, through the ministry of his priests.' (*A Catechism of Christian Doctrine*, 6–278: Catholic Truth Society, London 1985). Christ is the perpetual sacrifice, as represented by his still hanging on the crucifix. His words 'It is finished' do not mean that His sacrifice was finished, according to the Church of Rome; but that he had finished his earthly life and was now ready to offer himself as the perpetual victim or 'host'. The offering is for the sins of the living and the dead, and the wafer and wine are actually changed into the body and blood, the 'real presence' by the priest.

The Catholic Encyclopaedia defines this change, known as 'transubstantiation', as follows: 'In the Sacrament of the Eucharist the substance of bread and wine do not remain, but the entire substance of bread is changed into the body of Christ, and the entire substance of wine is changed into his blood, the species or outward semblance of bread and wine alone remaining. ... The dogma of the totality of the Real Presence means 'that in each individual species the whole Christ, flesh and blood, body and soul, Divinity and humanity, is really present.' (*The Catholic Encyclopedia*, vol. 4, p. 299 & vol. 14, p. 586)

When the priest consecrates the bread and wine, he uses the words of Matthew 26:26, 'hoc est corpus meum', 'this is my body.' In offering up the wafer, which now 'has become the whole Christ', he is seen to be sacrificing Christ.

What did the Reformers have to say about the Mass? Luther, a former priest of the Church of Rome, described it as 'an unspeakable abomination, quite contrary to the principal article of justification by faith alone.' Calvin called it 'Satan's attempt to adulterate and envelop the sacred Supper of Christ as with thick darkness.'

Cranmer was no less forthright; 'For these be but false doctrines, without shame devised and feigned by wicked popish priests, idolators, monks and friars, which for lucre have altered and corrupted the most holy Supper of the Lord and turned it into manifest idolatry. Wherefore all godly men ought with all their heart to refuse and abhor all such blasphemy against the Son of God.'

The Council of Trent gave the Reformers the Roman Catholic reply. Uncompromising, it stands today, having been endorsed by the *Second Vatican Council (1962–65)*, which altered style, not substance;

'If anyone shall say that in the Mass there is not offered to God a true, proper and propitiatory sacrifice for the living and the dead, or what is offered is nothing else than Christ given to be eaten' i.e. transubstantiation, 'let him be anathema. ... If anyone shall say that in these words, "This do in remembrance of Me" ... let him be anathema.'

There is a need to emphasise that there has been no change in essence in the Mass since the Council of Trent. A Catholic Truth Society 1985 booklet 'How the Mass came to be', confirms this; 'Thanks to the Second Vatican Council and Pope Paul VI, we have a new liturgy today. But with all the changes, what we have is truly the Mass of Christ. What has changed is the manner of its celebration, the liturgy. For there can never be a new Mass. Vatican II held that the language of the Mass had changed, not the substance.'

The 'Blessed Sacrament'

A 1988 booklet, also published by the Catholic Truth Society, explains the special significance for Catholics of the 'blessed sacrament'; 'Communion for the sick is still the primary purpose for the reservation of the sacrament in our churches, but it is only natural that once reserved for that purpose, the sacramental presence of the Lord should be revered and adored. Our worship of Christ by focusing on the exposed sacrament should always lead us to a deeper love for the actual celebration of the Eucharist and to a more fruitful reception in communion of the body and blood of the Lord. At its heart, the Eucharist is the same yesterday, today, and for ever.'

The Catholic concept of the sacrament and the Eucharist is illustrated in the description given by Mother Teresa of Calcutta in one of her meditations. 'It is beautiful to see the humility of Christ ... in his permanent state of humility in the tabernacle, where he has reduced himself to such a small particle of bread that the priest can hold him with two fingers.' (*In The Silence of the Heart* by Mother Teresa, 1983)

Cardinal John Henry Newman, nineteenth century theologian, described by Popes Paul VI and John Paul II as the man who inspired the Second Vatican Council, placed his supreme trust in the blessed sacrament. 'When you think everything is gone from you,' he said in 1875, after the death of his friend Fr Ambrose St John, 'if you have with you Our Lord in the Blessed Sacrament, you still have everything.'

Shortly before the Lord Jesus shared the Last Supper with His disciples, He prophesied about deception and false

Christs. In what has become known as the Olivet Discourse, given on the Mount of Olives, He gave an unmistakeable warning;

> 'If any man shall say unto you, Lo, here is Christ, or there; believe it not.'

Jesus took bread in the upper room to symbolize His broken body. He did not take a round wafer. Alexander Hislop, author of the *The Two Babylons*, which was first published fully in 1858 and yet has not aged in content, argues that 'the "round" wafer, whose "roundness" is so important an element in the Romish Mystery, is only another symbol of Baal or the sun.' Hislop notes that 'it is striking to find that the image of the sun was erected *on high, above* the altars in the worship of Baal, as practised by the idolatrous Israelites in the days of their apostasy.' (2 Chronicles 34:4)

In his book *Babylon Mystery Religion*, Californian author, Ralph Woodrow, describes the huge altar in St Peter's Cathedral in Rome and the four ninety-five feet columns that support it. At the top of each column is a sun-image like those that were used in pagan worship. High on the wall also is a very large and elaborate golden sunburst image, just as there was in the great temple of Babylon. The sunburst images are also like the monstrance sun-image, in which the 'host' is placed as a 'sun' and before which Catholics kneel and bow.

Similar sun-images have been discovered above the altar in temples excavated to reveal the Egypt of the Pharoahs. Inscriptions found on the temple walls have demonstrated that the thin round cakes of the ancient mysteries were to be found on every altar. Hislop identified the cakes as those offered to the Queen of Heaven, 'the unbloody sacrifice' required by the Goddess Mother and offered to her by the Israelites. (Jeremiah 7:18.)

'The round disk, so frequent in the sacred emblems of Egypt, symbolized the sun', wrote Hislop. 'Now, when Osiris, the sun divinity became incarnate, and was born, it was not merely that he should give his life as a sacrifice for men, but that he might be the life and nourishment of the souls of men. ... Now, this Son, who was symbolized as "Corn", was the Sun divinity incarnate, according to the sacred oracle of the great goddess of Egypt: "No mortal has lifted my veil. The fruit which I have brought forth is the **sun**". What more natural then, if this incarnate divinity is symbolized as *the bread of God*, than that he should be represented as a *round wafer* to identify him with the Sun?' (*The Two Babylons* by Revd Alexander Hislop – Section III, The Sacrifice of the Mass: Loizeaux Brothers, Neptune, New Jersey; *Babylon Mystery Religion* by Ralph Woodrow, Chapter 17: Ralph Woodrow Evangelistic Association, Riverside, California 92502)

The Burning Issue

Protestants, (or those who profess the inerrancy and total authority of the Scriptures), see the Mass as contrary to Scripture, in particular in the book of Hebrews:

> *But this man, after he had offered **one** sacrifice for sins for ever, sat down on the right hand of God.*
>
> Hebrews 10:12.

> *And as it is appointed unto men once to die, but after this the judgment: So Christ was once offered to bear the sins of many; and unto them that look for Him shall He appear the second time without sin unto salvation.*
>
> Hebrews 9:27

These two verses summarize the total **once and for all** saving work of the atonement. The 28th of the 39 articles of the Church of England (1571) declares: 'Transubstantiation is repugnant to the plain words of Scripture, overthroweth the nature of a sacrament and hath given occasion to many superstitions. The sacrament of the Lord's Supper was not by Christ's ordinance reserved, carried about, worshipped, nor was it lifted up.'

Contrast this with Pope John XXIII's account of a Mass he attended before Vatican II; 'Our voice trembling with emotion ... the central, guiding and shining point of that meeting. Our consecrated and blessed hands raised aloft the Eucharistic Sacrifice, Jesus, our Saviour and Redeemer' (*Journal of a Soul*, Pope John XXIII, letters and writings)

Martin Luther considered that the 'Babylonian captivity of the Church' 'consisted in the denial to the laity of Communion in both kinds, (bread and wine) and in the doctrines of Transubstantiation and the Sacrifice of the Mass.' (Oxford Dictionary of the Christian Church)

The English Reformers flatly denied the doctrine of the real presence of Christ in the Mass, and insisted on the key words 'in remembrance of me' of 1 Corinthians 11:24. and for that reason many of them were burned at the stake. The English Reformation centred around this very issue. One after another, Rogers, Bradford, Bishops Hooper, Latimer and Ridley, Archbishop Cranmer; all went to their deaths denying a doctrine which they felt damaged and obscured the whole system of Christ's truth. They knew the importance to posterity of their stand.

When the Banner of Truth Trust re-published *Five English Reformers*, abridged in 1960 from Bishop J.C. Ryle's 1890 classic, *Light From Old Times*, the Publishers of the Banner were themselves moved to write an introduction which brought a sobering message, part of which is reproduced here. It includes a solemn warning about the re-establishing of the Mass from the great evangelical Bishop, and a prediction already fulfilled.

'While we sleep, an onslaught is being mounted against us, an onslaught which the Protestant churches of our land were never less ready to sustain. Anglican and Nonconformist leaders alike have thrown away the only weapon that could defend us – "the sword of the Spirit", the Infallible Word of God. *The Word of God alone, the grace of God alone, the power of the Spirit alone*, these were the watch cries which prevailed four hundred years ago. They are not the watch cries of our Protestant pulpits today. J.C. Ryle, the first Bishop of Liverpool, as a student in Oxford in the 1830s witnessed the commencement of the Romeward movement in the Church

41

of England, and he lived long enough to see the stream become a flood – a flood which as he prophesied in his old age might in the next century carry all before it. Ryle's convictions on this subject were thought out over a long period; he was no hasty alarmist, but he watched Rome's power grow, he read and reread our Church history, he knew human nature, and he spoke accordingly: "A sapping and a mining process has been long going on under our feet, of which we are beginning at last to see a little. *We shall see a good deal more by and by*. At the rate we are going, it would never surprise me if within fifty years the crown of England were no longer on a Protestant head, and High Mass were once more celebrated in Westminster Abbey and St Pauls." It is solemn to note that on 2nd February 1960, a service of Requiem Mass was held for the late Earl of Halifax at Westminster Abbey.'

(*Five English Reformers*: Banner of Truth, Feb.1960)

Ryle argued that 'the Romish doctrine of "the real presence", if pursued to its legitimate consequences, obscures every leading doctrine of the Gospel, and damages and interferes with the whole system of Christ's truth. It produces an idolatry to be abhorred of faithful Christians.' (*Why Were Our Reformers Burned?: Five English Reformers* by J.C. Ryle, Banner of Truth)

Did the Apostle Paul deal with the problem for us today as well as for the Corinthians of his day in his second letter?; '*And what agreement hath the temple of God with idols? For ye are the temple of the living God. .... Wherefore, come out from among them and be ye separate, saith the Lord, and touch not the unclean thing; and I will receive you.*' (2 Corinthians 6:16,17)

The writer to the Hebrews reminded them that Jesus Christ has an '*unchangeable priesthood*'. He needs not '*daily as those high priests, to offer up sacrifice, first for His own sins, and then for the peoples, for this He did ONCE, when He offered up Himself.*' (Hebrews 7:24, 27)

It was scriptures like these and Revelation 18:4, '*Come out of her my people, that you be not partakers of her sins, and that you receive not of her plagues'* that brought about and motivated the Protestant Reformation.

What then of 'the expression of the Renewal in Eucharistic celebrations' – the new enthusiasm for the Mass among Charismatic Catholics? Does it represent hope for unity in the Church or is it rather the flickering of Hugh Latimer's candle, lit by the Reformers and now in danger of extinction?

The Re-establishing of the Mass

In October 1988 the Lord Chancellor, Lord Mackay, was suspended as an elder of his church, the Free Presbyterian Church of Scotland, for attending two separate Requiem Masses for his friends. The Kirk's position, represented editorially as one of 'almost unbelievable bigotry' (*Sunday Express*, 16th October 1988), is in fact the constitutional position of the Queen and Royal Family. The BBC, in their programme coverage, referred frequently to 'the principle' that had motivated the Kirk; but that principle did not find expression or obtain definition in most of the media.

There has been considerable concern about Prince Charles' attendance at a Mass in September 1986 at Kirkby Stephen in Cumbria with his friends Hugh and Emily van Cutsem. Earlier as heir to the throne he was prevented by command of the Queen from participating in the Pope's private mass at the Vatican. The Prince of Wales also attended a mass during his visit to Normandy for the commemoration of the landings.

Until this century, the Mass had been outlawed for the sovereign and his heirs in the Coronation Oath, which was designed to place both king and country under the authority of the Holy Bible. It was in 1910, and a decade before home rule for Eire, that an Asquith government, clinging to office and under pressure from the Irish Nationalists as well as the sacerdotalists in the Anglican church, removed the offending 1689 wording which prohibited the Monarch and the heirs to the throne from any exposure to the Mass. At his coronation George V's Oath would have included: '... I, George, do solemnly and sincerely, in the presence of God,

43

profess, testify and declare that I do believe that in the Sacrament of the Lord's Supper there is not any Transubstantiation of the Elements of Bread and Wine into the Body and Blood of Christ, at or after the consecration thereof by any person whatsoever; and that the Invocation or Adoration of the Virgin Mary or any other Saint, and the Sacrifice of the Mass, as they are now used in the Church of Rome, are superstitious and idolatrous.'

This safeguard, as it surely was intended to be, is in keeping with Archbishop Cranmer's solemn warning to the church about the Mass:

> 'What availeth it to take away beads, pardons, pilgrimages and such other like popery, so long as the two chief roots remain unpulled up? So long as they remain, there will spring up the former impediments of the Lord's harvest, and corruption of the flock. The rest is but branches and leaves, the cutting away whereof is like topping and lopping of a tree, or cutting down the weeds, leaving the body standing and the roots in the ground. But the very body of the tree, or rather the roots of the weeds is the popish doctrine of Transubstantiation, of the real presence of Christ's flesh and blood in the sacrament of the altar (as they call it) and of the sacrifice and oblation of Christ made by the priest for the salvation of the quick and the dead. Which roots, if they be suffered to grow in the Lord's vineyard, will overspread all the ground again with the old errors and superstitions.' (*The True and Catholic Use of the Lord's Supper*: Thomas Cranmer)

Attendance Then and Now

The 'principle' of the Free Presbyterians that the BBC spoke of, which is outlined in their 1989 booklet *Free Presbyterians and the Requiem Mass*, is a longstanding one. At the time of the Reformation, Protestant leaders would not agree to Christians attending the mass without making a protest against it.

Calvin had very firm views about attendance of the mass.

Reformed Christians in his day were in danger if they failed to attend, and many of them wanted to conceal the fact that they were Protestants. However Calvin strongly opposed the view that Protestants could attend mass while at the same time secretly disapproving of it in their hearts. Such action would not be worship but dishonour of God. The stakes were very much higher in those times and Calvin knew that his stand was endangering lives. Although it made him deeply unpopular, he still maintained 'on the strongest grounds, that Christian men ought not even to be present at the mass.' Calvin saw Paul's words to the Corinthians, *'flee from idolatry'* as the imperative from the Lord. (1 Corinthians 10:14)

This is in marked contrast to the approach of the charismatic renewal and the 'new evangelicalism' so prevalent in the Church today. In 1978, Dr Donald Coggan became the first Archbishop of Canterbury since the reign of Mary I to attend Papal Mass. Robert Runcie also attended a Papal Mass in Rome in October 1989, although it was made clear to him, by Vatican officials that he was not permitted to take Communion.

During the last two decades, there has been a new emphasis on sacramental worship, with the Mass regularly celebrated at Sunday services, and references to it on TV and in radio plays and documentaries as representative of Christian worship, have become a noticeable feature in our lives. Christmas 1990 offered viewers four televised services, of which three were Masses. Requiem Masses, including 'prayers for the dead' have frequently occupied centre stage at times of national tragedy and disaster. Thus the reinstatementment of the Mass in the public mind, and in the life of our nation, is becoming a reality in our day.

Chapter 3

The Virgin Mary

In his book, *A New Pentecost*, Cardinal Suenens wrote; 'Ecumenism has tended to play down Mary's role, but the Renewal Movement has marked out a place for her as "the first charismatic."'

In fact renewed 'Evangelical' churches have not been playing down Mary's role. On the contrary, many of them are also referring to her as 'the first charismatic', stressing her humanity, acknowledging 'the special role she played at Pentecost' and underlining her 'accessibility'. This 'redressing of the balance' or 're-instatement of Mary's important place in the Bible', in the strong ecumenical climate now prevailing, is confusing and troubling ordinary church members who wish to hold on to clear and firm Protestant roots.

Few 'evangelical' churches as yet are as convinced as Cardinal Suenens, who in *A New Pentecost* later recalls that 'a brief mention stressing the role of Mary at an International Charismatic Conference in 1973 was met with a standing ovation from some 20,000 persons. I felt like we were one family gathered in our home around our mother.'

Pope John Paul II's reference to England as 'Mary's Dowry' received a similar rapturous response at Wembley Stadium during the Papal visit in 1982. The Pope's observation reflects the unchanging Vatican position regarding the claim to Papal suzerainty over England which goes back to the time of King John. John Paul's kissing of the ground on arrival was the sign of the historic claim that this country belongs to Mary and the Mother Church. Professor Malachi

Pope John Paul II arrives in Wales.
© The Press Association, June 1982

Martin, who is described as a former Jesuit, and who worked closely with the present Pope in the Vatican, confirms that the practice of kissing the soil of each nation the Pope visits is to consecrate that country to Mary, to whose service he is dedicated.

The Queen of Heaven

Pius XII, a Pope many today still remember, described Mary as 'Queen of Heaven'. He it was, on November 1st 1950, who proclaimed 'infallibly', ex-Cathedra, 'that Mary's body was raised from the grave shortly after she died, and she was taken up and enthroned as Queen of Heaven.' At St Peter's Square on Easter Day 1988, Pope John Paul II's message included a prayer 'to the Queen of Heaven for protection and peace in the world.' The only references to be found in Scripture of the Queen of Heaven relate to the Canaanite pagan goddess to whom the Israelites burned incense, made cakes and poured out drink offerings and who was detestable and wicked in the eyes of the Lord. Jeremiah 44:17–25, 7:18.

In *The Two Babylons*, Alexander Hislop identifies the worship of the Queen of Heaven of the Bible with that of Semiramis, who was the wife of Nimrod and worshipped by the Babylonians; as well as with the worship of the Assyrian Goddess Astarte, of Diana of the Ephesians, of the virgin Venus in pagan Rome and of many other virgin mother goddesses all over the world. Semiramis' son, referred to in Scripture under the name of Tammuz (Ezekiel 8:14), who met a violent death and for whom the women wept, is identified with Osiris in Egypt and Bacchus in Rome. **Mother and child** were worshipped in the popular religion of Babylon, represented in pictures and images as an infant or child in his mother's arms. Likewise, after the tower of Babel, by many nations and peoples all over the world; in Egypt as Isis and Osiris; in India, to this day, as Isi and Iswara; in pagan Rome as Venus or Fortuna and Jupiter. Even in Tibet, China and Japan, the Jesuit missionaries were astonished to find the counterpart of Madonna and her child as devoutly worshipped as in Papal Rome itself; Shing Moo, the Holy Mother in China, being represented with a child in

48

her arms, and a glory around her, exactly as if a Roman artist had been employed to set her up. (Revd Alexander Hislop: *The Two Babylons*, Loizeaux Bros., Neptune, New Jersey)

Pius IX, whose contribution to the Church has been especially singled out for veneration by the present Pope, described Mary as 'Mary, Mother of God, who has destroyed all heresies throughout the world and who allows herself to be entreated by all, shows herself to be most clement towards all, and takes under her pitying care all our necessities with most ample affection, sitting as Queen upon the right hand of her only begotten Son our Lord Jesus Christ, in a golden vestment clothed around with various adornments.' (Encyclical letter, December 1864)

Certainly the flavour of such descriptions belongs more to Jeremiah's prophecy than to the New Testament.

Many photographs appear in the press of the present Pope praying in front of statues or images of the Virgin Mary. One such picture, in the *Daily Telegraph*, was of 'the Pope descending Mount Chetif in North West Italy after climbing to the summit to pray at a statue of the Virgin Mary.' (*Daily Telegraph*: 8th September 1986)

Former Member of Parliament Geoffrey Cooper pointed out the Scripture in the Gospel of John, in which Jesus said to the Samaritan woman; *'you shall neither worship on this mountain, nor yet at Jerusalem worship the Father . . . the true worshippers shall worship the Father in spirit and in truth: for the Father seeketh such to worship him.'* (John 4:21 & 23) Not on a mountain, not at Jerusalem, nor at Lourdes or Walsingham. There are no holy places, no special shrines, no holy water or sacred relics, no 'real presence'; God is omnipresent and within every believer, by His Spirit.

Mr Cooper's entirely biblical response and concern over the increasing promotion of pilgrimages and of Mary-worship has not yet found a voice within the press of this free nation.

Jesus Christ is not Mary's only begotten son, He is the only begotten Son of God. Nor is Mary, Mother of God. Nor indeed is she 'Mother of the Creator', 'Queen of Virgins', 'Ideal of Holiness', 'Throne of Knowledge', 'Source of our Joy', 'Queen of Peace', 'Rose of Heaven', 'Gate to Heaven',

'Radiant Tabernacle', 'Rock of David', 'Golden Temple', 'Morning Star', 'Haven of the Sinners', 'Consolation of the Afflicted', 'Queen of Angels', 'Queen of the Apostles', 'Queen of the Martyrs', 'Queen of Paradise' or 'Queen of Heaven'. (*Ricordi Religiosi*, Turin 1968)

Mary, has the honoured and distinguished place which Scripture accords her. 'All generations shall call her blessed.' But in no respect can she be elevated to occupy the place of Christ Himself. She was humble and obedient and she needed a Saviour, like the rest of mankind. Luke 1:47. He made things clear; *'whosoever shall do the will of my Father who is in heaven, the same is my brother and sister and mother.'* (Matthew 12:50) Mary did His will.

John Paul II and Mary

John Paul II has as his personal motto, 'totus tuus' (totally yours); but it applies to Mary, not Jesus. Indeed at his enthronement he proclaimed '. . . all that I have is thine, my Queen and my Mother.' After the attempt on his life in 1981, *Time Magazine* reported under the heading 'It's Like Shooting God', that on his way to hospital, 'he softly murmured 'Madonna, Madonna' in Polish'. (*Time*: 25th May 1981). One year after the assassination attempt, he went to the Marian shrine of Fatima in Portugal to thank Mary for saving his life. More details of the part the Pope believes Our Lady of Fatima played in saving his life and will play in his future follow on when we look at the importance of Fatima later on in this chapter.

In April 1987 the Pope launched the 'Marian Year' to a global TV audience estimated, perhaps generously, at 1.5 billion. Two months later, at a Mass for several hundred thousand people at Lodz in Poland, he prayed to the Virgin Mary for religious freedom in the world. In May 1988, in the Cathedral at Lima, he consecrated Peru to 'Our Lady of Evangelization', anticipating the *Decade of Evangelization* to follow. In Rome, in August 1988, in a ceremony to mark the end of the Marian Year, the Pope proclaimed; 'This is the opportunity to start a Marian walk towards the year 2000. We must walk together with Mary.' He was speaking in Italian on that occasion. (*Famiglia Cristiana Magazine*: Piedmont, Italy).

The International magazine, *New Evangelization 2000*, published by Tom Forrest in the Vatican to promote the Decade of Evangelization, featured the Madonna with child as the front-piece to its special January 1991 edition 'The Decade of Evangelization Begins'. An earlier edition reprinted the Pope's Angelus Prayer of 'Mission Sunday', October 23rd 1988; 'May Mary be the model to which People of God look in order to live out their missionary commitment. Let us ask her with trust to intercede with her son to obtain for the Church a new Pentecost, a new Missionary Advent for the Jubilee Year 2000 and for the beginning of the third Millennium of the Christian Faith.'

In the U.S.A. the Papal visit and the enormous publicity generated by it, added currency to the claim made for Mary's 'special place', her role as an intercessor and her share in the divinity of her Son. Here in Europe, we can see a similar picture emerging. Pilgrimages to the Marian shrines at Lourdes, Fatima, Knock, Medjugorje and Walsingham, widely advertised in the press and featured on television, attract millions of worshippers from all over the world.

The Shrine of *Our Lady of Czestochowa* with its famous image of the Black Madonna, has played its part, very visibly among all the great events reported from Poland in the International press during the last few years. Lech Walesa's photograph with the image has been widely syndicated and the Pope has twice visited the shrine which is about 200 kilometres away from his home town of Cracow.

Walsingham and Mary

'Our Lady of Walsingham', parent shrine to 180 other shrines in Church of England churches, was host in September 1988 to the BBC programme 'Songs of Praise' watched by up to 8 million viewers. 1988 has seen a special pilgrimage organised for some sixty Bishops from the Lambeth Conference as well as the third consecutive pilgrimage from Parliament. Encouraged by the example of former Archbishop of Canterbury, Robert Runcie, senior bishops turn

The statue of the Virgin Mary from the shrine of Our Lady of Walsingham being carried to be blessed by Pope John Paul II.
© The Press Association, May 1982

out to lead the pilgrimage year after year. Archbishop Runcie, who was President of the *Ecumenical Society of the Blessed Virgin Mary*, and who, according to *Time magazine*, was 'probably willing to risk more for the sake of unity than any of his predecessors', was 'an enthusiast for Walsingham and its role in leading the Anglican Church into Catholicism of the Roman kind.' (*Time magazine*: 7th June 1982)

Walsingham worship includes the procession of a statue of the Virgin Mary, the processing and adoration of the host or blessed sacrament, blessing with 'holy water' and the veneration and kissing of a 'relic of the true cross'.

Those who question Catholic Renewal point also to the renewed enthusiasm among many charismatics for the rosary, with its repetitious 'Hail Marys' and ten times as many prayers to Mary as to God the Father and none to Christ. Certainly there are no obvious signs that the worship of Mary has been effectively slowed down by the Renewal. On the contrary, new doctrines are under discussion and indications are that a new proclamation about her may be forthcoming soon. Mary Mediatrix and Co-redemptrix are already falling into the new tradition of this century. 'As no man goes to the Father except by the Son, so no man goes to the Son except by His Mother.' (*Papal Encyclical 1897*). Vatican II declared Mary 'Mother of the Church'. In his March 1987 encyclical 'Redemptoris Mater', the Pope explained that 'while Mary is in no sense a mediator between God and man, which is Christ's role alone, ... she constantly precedes the Church in her journey through human history and co-operates with Christ's work of salvation.' (*The Universe*, 27th March 1987)

The Marian Cult

The dogma of the Assumption and the Immaculate Conception of the Virgin Mary, both of which are relatively recent additions to Tradition, have been established quickly in the Roman Church. Such is the ecclesiastical weight of Papal decree and the discipline of the whole institution.

The Marian cult is not part of the ARCIC or other ecumenical discussions. Catholic devotion to Mary is not

53

negotiable. The strength of reaction to Neil Kinnock's speech of 9th April 1989 with its intended humour relating to the 'immaculate misconception' and 'the Assumption of the Blessed Margaret', clearly underlined just how important Mary is to Catholics in Britain. Bishop Alan Clark of East Anglia wrote to Opposition leader Kinnock of 'the offence given by the completely insensitive use of one of the central beliefs of the Catholic faith.' Cardinal Hume also wrote a 'strongly worded letter' stressing the importance to the Catholic faith of the doctrines of the Assumption and the Immaculate Conception. (*Catholic Herald*: 14th April 1989).

It was noted that the indignation and the 'wave of protests from Catholic Church leaders all over the country' over this insult to Mary was quite different from the restrained, dignified and statesmanlike reaction of the Catholic leadership to the showing of the highly controversial and blasphemous film *Last Temptation of Christ*.

Unity and Mary

The Pope proclaimed in 'Redemptoris Mater' that 'Mary will help lead Christians to unity,' but there seems to be a picture emerging that Mary may be the means for the uniting of **all** faiths under one umbrella.

Ecumenical dialogue between Roman Catholicism and Islam is taking place in many non-Protestant countries. The shrine of Fatima in Portugal, of great prophetic importance to Catholics, has also become important to Muslims. It is very often equated or confused with Fatimah, the daughter of Muhammad, of whom the prophet wrote, 'She is the most holy of all women in Paradise, next to Mary.' (*The Woman Shall Conquer* by Don Sharkey: Franciscan Marytown Press, Wyoming USA)

Muriel Spark relates that at Medjugorje in Yugoslavia, some two months after the apparitions began in September 1981, Muslims joined with Orthodox and Catholics in the pilgrimages. Devout Catholics were deeply shocked. The Madonna is reported as saying 'God is indivisible, it is not God but believers who have caused the dreadful divisions in the world.' In the ecumenical spirit of our day, she is said to have pointed out that devout Catholics seem to go out of their way to avoid contact with Orthodox and Moslems; yet nobody who refused to take other believers seriously was worthy of the name of Christian.

By way of underlining this difficult message, 'Our Lady' singled out a Moslem woman called Pasha, for special praise. 'She is a true believer, a saintly woman. You should be more like her.' A priest who had expressed scepticism about one of the claimed healings was corrected by the Lady; 'Tell that priest and others like him that it is they who are perpetuating the divisions in the world. Muslims, Orthodox, Catholics, to my Son and myself all are one. You are all my children.' Clearly the Madonna has no time for the 'separated brethren'; but it is easy to see why there is so much controversy within the Roman Church relating to the authenticity of the Madonna's appearances at Medjugorje. (Muriel Spark: *Spark from Heaven* p 85)

'Mary, the Mother, unquestionably has global appeal. She is alluring not only to Catholics, but represents a syncretistic goddess who is able to unite all faiths, for her motherhood stirs the deepest yearnings of the human spirit ... Indeed when a "Pilgrim Virgin", a statue of Our Lady of Fatima, toured Africa and Asia, millions flocked to venerate the statue and learn of Our Lady's "Peace Plan from Heaven." Muslims, Buddhists, Hindus and Sikhs were particularly enthusiastic. The Muslims, who have a certain devotion to Our Lady and recognize her Virgin Birth and Immaculate Conception, were intrigued by the fact that Mary had appeared at Fatima, which was the name of Muhammad's favourite daughter and regarded by the prophet as the highest woman in Heaven after Our Lady. .. The Muslim chief of the Ismaeli tribe in Mozambique placed a golden necklace about the statue's neck, saying, "Thank you, Our Lady of Fatima for the work of love you are accomplishing in Africa. We praise you, together with the Almighty Allah."' (*National Research Institute – Trumpet*, November/ December 1990: 3140K S. Aurora, Colorado 80014)

According to Mariologist John Haffert, more than 100,000 people witnessed the 'miracle' of Fatima on 13th October 1917, although other writers estimate the number as nearer

70,000. This was the sixth reported appearance of 'Our Lady of Fatima', who had appeared on the 13th day of each month that summer since 13th May to three Portuguese children; Lucia, aged 8, Jacinta, aged 6 and Francisco, also aged 8; and had promised to perform a miracle in October 'so that all may believe'. Witnesses to what took place on that day, were terrified by what they saw and hesitant and fearful in describing it afterwards. Apparently the sun at first appeared as a 'silver disk' and then suddenly a spectrum of multi-coloured light shot out in every direction and the sun appeared to spin madly on its axis 'like a gigantic wheel of fire', splashing its hues of red, yellow, blue and green on the rocks and trees and upturned faces of the astonished pilgrims. Three times it stopped and then it resumed its 'mad dance'. Then, as the crowd cringed in 'abject terror', the sun suddenly seemed to be torn loose from the firmament. Down, down, down it plunged, zig-zagging dizzily through the sky. Wails of 'It's the end of the world!' and 'Dear Lady, save us!' arose from the terrified multitude. Then as suddenly as it had begun, the sun stopped its gyrations and returned to its post in the sky. As the trembling crowd recovered from its fright, cries of astonishment arose: their garments which had been soaked and mud-covered, from the pelting rain that they had endured before the miracle, were miraculously dry!

During the spectacle, 'Mary' is said to have appeared, holding a Rosary and Scapular and identified herself as 'Our Lady of the Rosary' and asking that the Rosary be prayed every day. In July, she had given the Church her directive for a 'world devotion and for the consecration of Russia to her immaculate heart.' She is also quoted as saying that 'many, many souls are going to hell, **because there is no one to make sacrifices for them**.' (C. Borden Lindstedt: *NRI Trumpet*, November/December 1990)

A remarkable revelation from a 1990 book, *The Keys of This Blood*, written by Professor Malachi Martin, who is described as a former Jesuit, is that Pope John Paul II believes in his own special destiny as directed by Our Lady of Fatima. He is convinced that he will be called in the 1990s to be the moral and spiritual leader of a world government. He is also sure that it was Our Lady of Fatima who spared his life from the assassination attempt on 13th May 1981, for it was as he bent over to inspect an 'Our Lady of Fatima' medal, worn by a little girl, on the Anniversary of the first Fatima appearance, that the two shots specifically aimed at his head passed over him. While he was recovering from the assassination attempt, which had taken place on the official feast day of Our Lady of Fatima, he had a vision of things to come. In the vision, which apparently came from prayer and his total trust in Our Lady of Fatima, and was as an exact repetition of what had taken place at Fatima on 13th October 1917, the Virgin Mother told him that there would be a repeat of the Fatima miracle. She will intervene in the 1990s with signs and wonders, again involving the sun, which will authenticate John Paul's reign over the world ... for a short time of peace and prosperity before the return of Christ. (Malachi Martin: *The Keys of This Blood*, 1990, Simon and Schuster, New York)

In 1982, in obedience to the Fatima directive and with the 'Collegial consensus of the Bishops of the world,' Pope John Paul II reconsecrated Russia and the entire world to 'the immaculate heart of Mary.'

In May 1991, John Paul made his third Papal visit to Fatima to again thank the Virgin Mary for saving his life, to tell the world how much the 'Mother of God' is needed, and that any 'renewal' of the world could only take place in such a context. (*The Universe*: Sunday 19th May 1991)

Chapter 4

Tradition

In examining the subject of 'Holy Tradition', it would be helpful first for the reader to appreciate the extent to which the individual Roman Catholic is bound by 'confession of faith' to subscribe to all that is added to Scripture by the Church. Such confession includes the following:

> 'I admit and embrace most firmly the apostolic and ecclesiastical traditions and all the other constitutions and prescriptions of the Church. ... Besides I accept without hesitation, and profess all that has been handed down, defined and declared by the Sacred Canons and by the general Councils, especially by the Sacred Council of Trent and by the Vatican General Council, and in a special manner concerning the primacy and infallibility of the Roman Pontiff. ... This same Catholic Faith, outside of which nobody can be saved, which I now freely profess and to which I truly adhere, the same I promise and swear to maintain and profess ... until the last breath of life.' (*Roman Catholic Catechism*: Geiermann, pp 101–103)

The confession from the Catechism adds to Scripture, which is expressly forbidden by Scripture. Swearing to the catechism is also forbidden by Scripture.

> *'Ye shall not add unto the word that I command you, neither shall ye diminish aught from it.'*
>
> Deuteronomy 4:2

'But above all things, my brethren, swear not, neither by heaven, neither by the earth, neither by any other oath: but let your yea be yea; and your nay, nay; lest ye fall into condemnation.'   James 5:12

The Council of Trent gave Tradition equal authority to the Bible itself, and without doubt much is added to the Word of God. Vatican II reminded Catholics that 'the Church does not draw her certainty about all revealed truths from the holy scriptures alone' (*Vatican II, Constitution on Divine Revelation* – para 9). The leading American Ecumenical magazine, *New Covenant*, reminded its readers in January 1987: 'Vatican II documents teach that both scripture and Tradition must be accepted and honoured with equal feelings of devotion and reverence.'

What does the Bible say about the tradition of men? Paul warned the Colossians; *'Beware lest any man spoil you through philosophy and vain deceit, after the tradition of men, after the rudiments of the world, and not after Christ.'* (Colossians 2:8)

Concerned evangelicals, including many in the Ecumenical Movement, have looked keenly to the Renewal to challenge that tradition of Councils and decrees that supplements or supersedes the Scriptures, but so far they have looked in vain. Visibly, at least, Catholicism is not in ferment; nor are its institutions and dogmas under seige. According to her Catechism, the Roman church alone is the one true Church that Christ founded, the chief attributes of which are authority, infallibility and indefectibility. (*Baltimore Catechism*: 1969 Catholic Book Publishing Co. NY)

'Semper Eadem', 'always the same'; Rome does not change her dogmas. She alters her style certainly but not her substance. Her face changes; she is very different in different countries. In England she adopts a high moral tone, represented in the Media as being firmer than that of any other part of the perceived Church. Cardinal Hume has emerged at the centre of our national life speaking with authority and clarity about the great moral issues of the day. Unpalatable Papal dogma such as *Humanae Vitae*, banning artificial contraception, is played down by the Church, while committed

Catholics lead Christians in the fight against the abortion legislation. The same Catholic leaders have founded the new Movement for Christian Democracy, 'an all-party, non-denominational organisation committed to bringing Christian values back into British political life.'

In countries where Roman Catholicism's grip is surer, standards do not rise so high. In Uganda, Haiti and the Philippines, to name but three in different parts of the world, Roman Catholicism is fully integrated into local paganism and the Gospel totally obscured within it. In the Philippines, missionaries regularly have a glimpse of the other face of Catholicism which is not to be seen in England. At Easter time young Filipinos do penance for 'serious' sins by being nailed to crosses and left to hang for several hours at a time. An article in *The Times* in 1987 described this dreadful tradition explaining that in this way the penitents believe that they obtain forgiveness from their god via his priest. (*The Times*: 18th April 1987)

In a number of countries in Africa and in Haiti, the local power of the priest is equated to that of the witch doctor or the voodoo 'god'. In primitive and superstitious cultures the Church exerts a stranglehold over all aspects of life, not dissimilar to that of the feudal system of medieval days. American author, Dave Hunt, tells us that Haiti is said to be '85% Catholic and 110% Voudun. Every voodoo ceremony begins with Catholic prayers. Likewise the deadly spiritist cult of Santeria is a blend of African witchcraft and Catholicism carried on in the name of the 'Saints' who front for African gods.' (Dave Hunt: *CIB Bulletin*, PO Box 7349, Bend OR 97708)

The pagan roots of Roman Catholic practice, described in Alexander Hislop's *The Two Babylons*, are widely accepted and even leading Catholics have been willing to acknowledge them. John Henry Newman, Rome's most famous English convert, did so comprehensively;

'The use of temples, and those dedicated to the particular saints, and ornamented on occasion with branches of trees, incense, lamps and candles; votive offerings on recovery from illness, holy water, asylums, holy days and seasons, use of calendars, processions, blessings on the fields, sacerdotal vestment, the tonsure, the ring in marriage, turning to the East,[1] images at a later date, perhaps the ecclesiastical chant and the Kyrie Eleison are all of pagan origin, and sanctified by adoption into the Church.' (Cardinal J.H. Newman: *An Essay on the Development of Christian Doctrine*, p 373)

This ritualistic facing of the east, equates both to Catholicism and to Freemasonry. For example a master mason of the third degree has to swear his oath of secrecy on *'The Volume of the Sacred Law'* facing east. The relationship between Catholicism and Freemasonry at the higher levels is discussed in the section on the Papacy and Political Power.

Some contemporary Protestants use up-to-date language to describe the Roman Catholic system and call it all a 'cult'. They are at pains to point out that they are referring to the institution and not to the spiritual standing of individuals within it. Apart from the pagan practices listed by Cardinal Newman, the research and scholarship of Hislop, Woodrow and others demonstrates the pagan origins also of the sacrificing Priesthood, penances, absolution and the Confessional, Papal Infallibility, the titles 'Holy Father' and 'supreme pontiff', the worship or veneration of Saints and relics (such as the Turin Shroud) and of idols, images, statues and symbols; stone altars; the rosary, the monstrance and wafer, prayers for the dead, extreme unction, purgatory and limbo, plenary indulgences,[2] ritualism, monasticism and mysticism; add to these pilgrimages, crosses and crucifixes, celibacy, the Mother and Child worship; Mary's continuing virginity, the scapular, canonization of Saints, Cardinals, nuns, the mitre (of Dagon, the fish-god), fish and Friday, the (mystic) 'keys', Lent (forty days of 'weeping for Tammuz' as in *Ezekiel 8:14*);

---

[1] *'Then said he unto me, Hast thou seen this, O son of man? turn thee yet again, and thou shalt see greater abominations than these. And he brought me into the inner court of the Lord's house, and, behold, at the door of the temple of the Lord, between the porch and the altar, were about five and twenty men, with their backs toward the temple of the Lord, **and their faces toward the east**; and they worshipped the sun toward the east.'* (Ezekiel 8:15, 16)

the sign of the cross, the 'Sacred Heart', Easter (from Astarte the goddess of spring, associated with the sun rising in the east), baptismal regeneration and justification by works; Peter 'the rock', rather than Peter's faith in Christ; all these things and many besides, are at the heart of modern Roman Catholicism. Not all are widely practised in Western Protestant countries, but they are nevertheless deeply embedded in Church tradition. All are unsupported by Scripture and many are expressly forbidden in the Bible.

---

[2] According to an article in the *Daily Telegraph* on 6th July 1986: 'Indulgences are now available on live TV and radio. Replays of the same programme won't do.' There are 70 officially listed ways of obtaining plenary indulgences. Such blessings are the responsibility of the Vatican department called the *Sacred Apostolic Penitentiary*, run by Monsignor de Magistris. The Church teaches that the living can obtain indulgences for the deceased by doing a work, such as praying the Rosary before the Blessed Sacrament or making the Stations of the Cross. Catholics who have come to a personal faith in Christ through the Scriptures, and many who haven't, may be shocked to discover that the source of knowledge for Catholic tradition, especially the Catechism, is often at odds with the Bible. An example of the most profound importance is the omission of the second commandment: *'Thou shalt not make unto thee any graven image or any likeness of anything that is in heaven above, or that is in the earth beneath. Thou shalt not bow down thyself to them, nor serve them.'* (Exodus 20:4 & 5)

Chapter 5

Ecumenical Dangers

[handwritten: → "The World Council of Churches"]

The dangers of doctrinal compromise for Evangelicals are compounded by the fact that the Greek Orthodox Church, a founder member of WCC, embraces largely the same traditions as Rome. Apart from the major disagreement in the past relating to Papal supremacy, there are few real differences in dogma between Roman, Greek and other Orthodox churches.

Since the introduction of the all-conquering *ASB (Alternative Service Book)*, in which the words of the Communion Service are almost identical to those used at the Roman Catholic Mass, Catholic doctrine within the Anglican church is encountering less and less resistance from Evangelicals. Anglo-Catholics are well organised at the national level and through organisations like *Church in Danger*, they have greatly assisted ecumenical progress. John Selwyn Gummer, a Cabinet Minister and a former very influential member of the Anglican Synod, spoke for the great majority of today's Anglo-Catholics: 'Our history, our religion, our civilization all stem from the common fount of Western Christendom. Our Roman Catholic brothers are working with us, under the inspired leadership of the Pope for the establishment of Christ's Kingdom.'

Ecclesia, the society for Anglo-Catholics in Britain, reacting to the prospect of women priests in the Church of England, argued in its newsletter that 'there are many who will decide that the Romeward path is the proper one in the event of an apostate Church of England.' The ascendancy of

Liberals in the Anglican leadership and their sympathy towards the multi-faith movement has distracted the attention of followers of Christ from what may prove to be the greater threat, that of counterfeit religion and the deception we are twice warned of by the Lord in Matthew 24:4 & 24. *'Then if any man shall say unto you, Lo, here is Christ, or there; believe it not. For there shall arise false Christs, and false prophets, and shall shew great signs and wonders; in so much that, if it were possible, they shall deceive the very elect.'*

The Ecumenists of ARCIC have contrived to bridge all doctrinal differences with the likely exception of the Infallibility of the Pope. Papal 'primacy' is seen as the likely compromise, which has already been taken on board by the leadership of the Anglican Church. The almost total abdication from the Reformed position of the Inter-Church Process is devastating and greatly weakens a Church already perceived to be in difficulties. Are the pagan traditions being renewed or discarded? Those honouring the memories of Cranmer, Latimer and Ridley who helped draft the Church of England's *Thirty Nine Articles* and who died for their Protestant faith, understandably seek to know, lest it all happen again. The prophetic Scriptures concerning the end time make clear that this is just what will happen and men and women will be called to die for their faith once again.

Many critics of Ecumenism predict that Church unity under the supremacy of Rome will rapidly lead to a fresh outbreak of bigotry and persecution. They believe that the behind-the-scenes political power of Catholicism is greatly underestimated already, and that when Church and State are reunited, such power will become irresistible.

Persecution of Protestants Today

In Protestant countries such as Britain and the USA, the Roman Church appears moderate and tolerant, but in Catholic countries such as Peru, Chile, Argentina, Columbia and Mexico, and countries in Africa like Uganda and Zambia, also short on experience with democracy but where the Catholic Church is strong, Rome's other side has shown itself in intolerance and cruelties towards Protestants.

The fact is that in such countries Protestant missionaries are being persecuted for their faith, and sometimes tortured and killed. Whether such happenings are represented as the excesses of Marxist insurgency or of *Liberation Theology*, if they surface at all, they certainly do not get proper reporting in the western press.

For example the slaughter of Evangelicals by fanatics in many different parts of Mexico in the 1950s was not dissimilar to the accounts that history has left us of the St Bartholomew's massacre of French Huguenot Protestants in the 16th century. The Mexican atrocities were reported at the time by the magazine *Tiempo*, a large circulation non-religious news magazine in Mexico City, and also by the Catholic newspapers, *Excelsior* and *Zocalo*. *Excelsior*, the Mexico City daily, reported that a 35 year-old preacher and his young companion, who were distributing Christian tracts, were stoned to death on 15th January 1989 by 'more than 100 angry Catholics.' None of the attackers has been arrested although the State government claims to have identified most of them. (*Christianity Today* 3rd March 1989)

At mid-day on Sunday 24 February 1991, a mob armed with cudgels, axes and machetes destroyed the homes of seventeen Presbyterian families of the Tzeltal Indian tribe of Southern Mexico, according to Presbyterian Pastor Pedro Arias. Reports from Amatenango del Valle, where the incident took place, revealed that the Roman Catholic group responsible said it intended to expel the Presbyterians from their town, stating they 'want nothing to do with Protestants.' Hundreds of evangelicals have been evicted from their lands in recent years over disputes regarding the practice of their faith, according to the *Evangelical Times*. (*Evangelical Times*: May 1991)

In Columbia, in 1948, a reactionary government attained power with the help of the Roman Catholic Church. A concordat was signed with the Vatican under which severe restrictions were placed on Protestants. From 1948 to 1959, 116 Protestants were killed, 66 Protestant churches or chapels were burned or bombed, and over 200 schools closed. (*Report of the Evangelical Confederation of Columbia*, Bulletin No. 50, June 26, 1959) The Vatican appeared to approve these things, for the Archbishop of Bogota was promoted to Cardinal by Pope John XXIII in 1960. (Lorraine Boettner: *Roman Catholicism*, Banner of Truth Trust, 1962)

Africa

The Fellowship of Christ's Disciples wrote in August 1990 of the difficulties evangelicals were experiencing in Kampala, the capital of Uganda, a country they describe as 'a Catholic stronghold':

> 'We are a group of disciples from different Pentecostal churches who meet daily for discipleship training. ... We are so excited because this country has a population of about 17 million of which about 50% are Roman Catholics. ... Here our days are numbered. This is the only time we can use to alert and warn the Body of Jesus Christ . Already the true believers have been banned by the Roman Catholic bishops from the media. They have such a big influence that they can even cause the government to do such a thing.' (*World-wide Gospel Outreach*, 2442 Cerrilos Road, Santa Fe, New Mexico.)

An evangelist in Zambia, whose name is withheld, wrote to *World-wide Outreach* in Sante Fe, New Mexico in much the same way:

> 'My country has plunged into misery. The Body of Christ is constantly facing onslaughts. It's true, Catholicism is ruling the land. Politics (social and spiritual aspects) have been sold to the Vatican. Every effort to evangelize is being thwarted. I wonder if you know that the Catholics, through their agents in Parliament have passed a law banning the formation of any other Christian ministry. ... Religious freedom is slowly declining and respect for the Pope is mounting.'

All of this seems to be paying major dividends for the Roman Church. During the Pope's 1990 tour of African countries, the press agency Reuters revealed that the number of Roman Catholics in Africa has grown from 55 million in 1980 to 79 million in 1990, and is expected to top 100 million by the end of the century.

Spain

It was only a quarter of a century ago in 1964 that in Spain a warehouse containing bibles of the British and Foreign Bible Society was burned down by the government authorities. At that time Protestants were debarred from holding any public office and the professions, such as medicine, nursing, law, teaching and banking, were for the most part closed to them. Protestant schools were banned, as were Protestant marriage services and funeral services in many towns. No Protestant literature could be published or distributed without a license.

Concerning the situation in Spain at that time, American sociologist Paul Blanshard wrote; 'The same Pope (John XXIII) who permits American bishops to declare in the United States that they favour the separation of Church and State in this non-Catholic country encourages his Spanish bishops to pursue a directly opposite policy in Catholic Spain. It is the Vatican and the Franco government that jointly deny to all Protestant churches and Jewish synagogues those liberties which leaders of the church in the United States profess to believe in.' (Paul Blanshard: pamphlet, *Ecclesiastical Justice in Spain*)

There has been improvement in the situation since Franco's Fascist regime was succeeded by the new Democracy. However, religious discrimination, often severe, still operates in many parts of Spain. It was only barely two years ago that Protestants were given access to the 'holy ground' of public cemeteries, usually owned or controlled by the Roman Catholic Church. Until then they had been required to bury their dead in public plots set aside for atheists, criminals or paupers.

In other predominantly Catholic countries with democratic traditions such as Italy, France (where Catholicism is mainly nominal), and the South of Germany, the Protestant minorities are very strongly opposed to the Ecumenical movement, although swimming against a very powerful tide. Hard won freedoms prevent persecutions today, but as we saw before and during the second war, the establishing of Fascist or totalitarian regimes can swiftly unleash religious persecution.

A letter written by the Pastor of an Evangelical church in central Italy to Church Society's *Cross and Way magazine*, published late in 1990, illustrates very well the Protestant perspective within a predominately Roman Catholic country:

> '... We believe that many of those who are in favour of this move (towards union with the Vatican) are unaware of the real nature of Roman Catholicism. Probably their own experience has been limited to contacts with official representatives of the Roman Catholic world while they remain almost totally ignorant of what it means to live in a country where it is the dominant religion.
>
> ... As regards the incredible influence which the Vatican has on society in Italy, the following is just the tip of the iceberg. The Roman Catholic Church openly supports the party of relative majority in the coalition government, dictating many of their decisions. During elections, Roman Catholics are openly directed from the pulpit to vote for the said party (Christian Democrats) and through the same party exert control over the most popular TV and radio channel on a national level. Thus millions of Italians have been indoctrinated by biased news coverage, the tragic situation in Northern Ireland being another obvious example.
>
> ... Whereas the Protestant Reformation has even today left its mark on society, those countries which remained under papal domination, like Italy, usually have one thing in common: an almost total lack of consideration for those who do not share their religious beliefs. Evangelical believers in Italy have little or no access to the media, often find their right of freedom of witness obstructed by the authorities while the Roman

Catholic Church enjoys total freedom and vast financial benefits from the State.'

The continuing persecution of tiny minorities of evangelicals by state Catholicism contrasts sharply with the benevolent tolerance extended to Catholics in Western Protestant countries. It was in Spain that the Inquisition carried out its worst excesses, but in many other parts of the world it has been extremely effective in controlling peoples and nations. Its Tribunal has never been abolished, nor has the Roman Church ever renounced physical force to obtain spiritual ends. There has never been any repentance or apology for the Inquisition. Where there is 'infallibility', real repentance is impossible.

The true church has always thrived under persecution and prospered among underprivileged minorities, The greatest threat to the grip of Roman Catholicism, and the ambitions of the Papacy, probably comes from the spectacular growth of the gospel in Latin America and Africa, and among the Hispanic and other less privileged Catholic communities in the United States.

Chapter 6

The Papacy and Political Power

Undoubtedly the profile of the Papacy is now rapidly rising. The public relations progress made by Roman Catholicism over the last few years has been remarkable. The post war reputation of the Vatican lay in ruins as a result of Pius XI's Concordats with Hitler, Mussolini and Franco and Pius XII's apparent sympathy with the Fascist cause and indifference to the plight of the Jews. An article in the London *Evening Standard* of 18th April 1989, by Irish Catholic statesman Connor Cruise O'Brien, argued that Pope Pius XI's earlier attempt to bring relief to the Jews was thwarted by his sudden death and by the subsequent opposition to the proposed measures of both his successor, Pius XII, and the Jesuit General, Ledochowski.[1]

Yet today the aura of media acclaim around the person of the Pope is quite remarkable and might even exceed that

---

[1] This article in *The Evening Standard* is exceptional. Many feature articles have appeared during the last three years in the quality newspapers and supplements, rehabilitating the reputation of Pope Pius XII. The rebuilding of this Pope's reputation is most important for Catholicism, as the Fatima cult has been greatly enhanced by his 'unique personal vision' of 1950, regarded by millions of the faithful as a special miracle of an extra-holy being. It was Pius XII also who declared and defined the doctrine of the Assumption of Mary in 1950, confirmed by his own mystical experience.

enjoyed by another Roman Catholic hero, first Catholic President of the United States John F. Kennedy, who came to power almost devoid of real policies and for much of the duration of his presidency enjoyed a unique prolonged honeymoon with the media.

Like John XXIII, John Paul II has demythologised and humanised the Papacy and his media performance has done much to remove suspicion and fear as well as unhappy memories. His background as an actor has been helpful in a world conditioned by images. His audience is not always able to distinguish real life from soap opera, and has largely relegated history to the status of the latter rather than the former.

In fact the present Pope's image and reputation appear unassailable. Vatican scandals involving large-scale fraud and corruption and complicity in a cover-up have simply been shrugged off. Archbishop Marcinkus, who was at the centre of it all, was protected by the Pope for more than seven years and the Italian state authorities somehow rendered helpless. According to *The Times* (18th July, 1987) 'in a surprise and almost unprecedented move, the Italian supreme court cancelled arrest warrants issued against Marcinkus and two other senior Vatican bankers.'

Roman Catholic Oxford Professor of Logic, Michael Dummett, accused the Pope of complicity in a cover up to protect Marcinkus. *The Sunday Telegraph* 15th March, 1987, reporting from the Catholic weekly, *The Tablet*, said that Prof. Dummett spoke of 'the Vatican Bank entangled with complicated practices from which the most pungent stink of corruption arises. These practices involved other banks, the Mafia and the seamiest type of Freemasonry, culminating in what was possibly the bizarre suicide, but more probably the grotesque murder of an Italian banker in London.'

The Catholic Herald reported that it had been revealed that Roberto Calvi was in London to seek help from Opus Dei. It is interesting that it has taken an Italian court ruling to judge Calvi's death as murder. Two inquests in London had previously determined an open verdict. The Italian judgment is a confirmation of the position adopted by Professor Dummett and also of Stephen Knight who in his book,

The Brotherhood argued that the death was 'inextricably bound up with the riddle of P2, and Freemasonry's penetration not only of the Roman Catholic Church but of the Vatican itself.' The Milan verdict has brought blunt accusations of complicity in Calvi's murder levelled at Marcinkus by Calvi's widow, who claims that her husband had told her shortly before his death: 'the priests want me dead.' Marcinkus resigned as head of the Vatican Bank, but remained under the Pope's protection and enjoyed Vatican immunity. Attempts by the Italian authorities to put him on trial with the others accused of fraud were brushed aside by the Vatican; the Pope simply refused to hand him over.

The Banco Ambrosiano fraud trial, seven years in the making and likely to last for one or two more, is taking place as this book is being written. According to the Sunday *Observer*, it is hoped that the trial will throw light on how a staggering £800 million vanished leading to the worst bank crash in post-war Europe: 'How deeply was the Holy See and its Polish Pope involved, and why? State investigators now believe that nearly £100 million was smuggled into Warsaw to help the Solidarity struggle and this is certain to be raised at the trial.' The article by William Scobie goes on to say that sources in the Vatican point out that they have a ready answer. If the Pontiff did support Walesa in this way, 'it has been the trip-wire for the freedom of all Eastern Europe.' (*The Observer*, Sunday 3rd June, 1990) The ends will have justified the means.

It seems likely that, apart from the transfer of funds to aid Solidarity and other Vatican ventures such as those in El Salvador and Nicaragua, also emerging will be the Vatican Bank's close dealings with the Mafia, centering around the colourful former drugs racketeer, Michele Sindona, close friend of Pope Paul VI, and with *P2 Masonic Lodge* Grand Master Lucio Gelli. The P2 Lodge connection is deeply embarrassing to the Roman Church. The influential P2, regarded by mainstream Freemasonry as something of a renegade, was expelled from Italian Masonry three years before the scandal broke. How was it then that the Vatican was so deeply involved with it? Disclosures could also be made, emerging out of the Vatican's involvement with P2 and Banco Ambrosiano, that funds were transferred, through a Vatican owned company called Bellatrix, to provide the means of supply of Exocet missiles to Argentina. To avoid such disclosures, Vatican 'watchman', Irishman Philip Power, has suggested, the Papacy would have seen the need for reconciliation or accomodation with Freemasonry. (*Irish Christian Assemblies*, Limerick, Ireland)

Just before the press revelations relating to the P2 Lodge of Italian Freemasonry and the Vatican Ambrosiano Bank scandal, the Papal ban on Freemasonry was suddenly lifted in January 1983. According to the widely acclaimed evidence gathered by author David Yallop, the involvement of leading members of the Roman Curia in secret societies, including P2 and other Masonic Lodges, was revealed to Pope John Paul I, by the Italian newsagency *L'Osservatore Politico*, shortly before his untimely and mysterious death in September 1978. 'Luciani (John Paul I) held the view that it was unthinkable for a priest to become a member of a Masonic Lodge. The "Great Vatican Lodge" list that the Pope was given contained the names of 121 confirmed members of Freemasonry to which the Roman Catholic Church had long declared itself implacably opposed.' (*In God's Name* p 255–6, D. Yallop 1984: Corgi Books).

Roman Catholic writer, Piers Compton, in his book *The Broken Cross*, recounts in considerable detail the initiation of Angelo Roncalli, later Pope John XXIII, into the society of Rose-Croix or Rosicrucians in 1935. He also lists eleven Cardinals, including Casaroli, Suenens and Villot; and 75 other senior prelates of the Church, Archbishops, Bishops, Monsignors and Papal Nuncios, together with their Code names and dates of Initiation as members of secret societies.

Masonry encourages all religions. 'The great architect of the universe' it is argued, can be approached through many mediators including Buddha, Muhammad, Krishna, or through Jesus Christ. Churches that accept Freemasonry offer little or no resistance to ecumenical unity, and thus Freemasonry and Catholicism, freed from the difficulties of the past, can share a common goal in overseeing one world faith.

Influence and Authority of the Papacy

Yet the Pope's moral authority continues to grow and he is recognised as a great leader. The influence he exercises in the world today is unrivalled since pre-Reformation times. A typical example of this is from an 1986 article in *Time Magazine*, about Zulu Chief Buthelezi; 'His prestige is such that he has conferred with Pope John Paul II, President Reagan, Prime Minister Thatcher and other world leaders.' During the hostage crisis in the Lebanon in August 1989, *The Times* reported that following the execution of American Colonel Higgins, President Bush consulted the Pope and other world leaders on the telephone. In November 1990, 'when President Gorbachev took the road to Rome,' as the *Daily Telegraph* put it, 'there was no more mockery of the size of the Pope's divisions; no more talk about the opium of the people . . . instead, a visit by the Pope to the Soviet Union would bring great prestige to the beleaguered president.' (*Daily Telegraph* 19th November, 1990) Mr Gorbachev was accompanied by 24 officials for that visit, a more powerful delegation than that accompanying him on his official visit to Italy.

The Vatican has enormous diplomatic clout and maintains one of the largest diplomatic representations of any country. Diplomatic relations with Britain and the United States have only very recently been established, in 1982 and 1984 respectively. (The first two US ambassadors to the Vatican, William Wilson and Frank Shakespeare were both members of the secret Knights of Malta, an organization which itself has diplomatic relations with no fewer than 42 nations). (*Concerned Christians*: 'Catholics and Charismatics': Denver Colorado).

No other 'Church' has ever seen the necessity for **any** involvement in such temporal activity. This uneasy mixture of confessional box and diplomatic bag has always posed problems for the national security of all countries. It has undoubtedly contributed to the problems in Nicaragua, El Salvador and particularly in Ireland. Yet the world's statesmen and rulers continue to seek audiences to consult the Pope on global strategy. George Schultz, America's Secretary of State, and like many key members of the Reagan administration, a Roman Catholic, consulted the Pope before major discussions, stopping off at the Vatican on the way to Middle-East peace conferences. Yasser Arafat, after the American acceptance of the December 1988 PLO peace initiative at the United Nations, also stopped at the Vatican on 24th December, 1988, presumably for more than a Christmas blessing. Arafat has met with the Pope more than once: two men with apparently very little in common.

It was significant that the 70-year breach of relations between the Kremlin and the Vatican was ended in December 1989 by President Gorbachev's going to the Vatican. It was Gorbachev's first call en route to his summit with President Bush. The Protestant Alliance's *Reformer* magazine sounded a warning:

> 'It is not without significance that Mikhail Gorbachev went to see the Pope in this time of crisis. This stirs fears in many hearts. The reunion of Germany under a Vatican dominated party gives cause for concern. Will history be repeated? Will there be a pro-Vatican bloc in Europe again, this time allied to a friendly Russia, with Poland, Hungary, Romania and Czechoslovakia in tow? Will this be a repeat on a wider scale of the Vatican's support of the central powers leading up to the First World War and the Fascist powers in the Second World War? These are pertinent questions, the Vatican has never lost its objective of world dominion!'

Poland and the Papacy

The Sunday Express banner headline on 6th November 1988, 'Maggie Sought Pope's Blessing' revealed that Mrs Thatcher took the extraordinary step of consulting the Pope on the eve of her spectacular visit to Poland.

At Lodz in Poland in 1987, the Pope illustrated the Vatican's new clout in the Communist world, when he told a huge assembly of workers at an open-air Mass that they had the right to be represented by free trade unions.

Lech Walesa, newly elected President of Poland and Nobel Peace prize-winner, described by the press as a 'fervent Catholic', seems to have led a charmed life, all through the heady days of the launch and 'struggle' of Solidarity. He thrived while the trade union grew during the Communist years, moving freely around the world, with his meteoric career culminating in his election as Head of State in December 1990. His closeness to all things Catholic is apparent for everyone to see.

The Evening Standard, in an editorial on 29th November 1989, described Walesa as 'a man of enormous power in Poland ... He is not a politician, not a soldier, not exactly a trade unionist. He is a Catholic first; a Polish nationalist second; and if he is a socialist at all, it is only in that he is not an avowed capitalist.'

He is regularly photographed with crucifixes or with images of the Virgin Mary, or making the sign of the cross on TV; also with Cardinals and priests who previously acted as mediators with the Communist government. *The Associated Press* reported on 11th of December, 1990, that Walesa publically swore allegiance to the Black Madonna of Jasna Gora, also known as Our Lady of Czestochowa.[2]

His close relationship with the Church of Rome may well explain the freedom that Lech Walesa enjoyed in the early years of Solidarity, as well as indicate the extent of the influence exercised for many years by the Vatican over the Communist regime. This freedom is reminiscent of the remarkable liberty that John Paul II himself had enjoyed as Cardinal Wojtyla before he became Pope. It was very apparent at that time that the same freedom was not extended to the Primate of that time, Cardinal Wyszynski. The French publication *Didasco* expressed its scepticism soon after John

---

[2] Malachi Martin, in his book *The Keys of This Blood*, emphasizes the Pope's devotion to the Black Virgin of Jasna Gora. Martin claims that John Paul believes the Virgin of Jasna Gora was the chief reason that he was elected Pontiff. Dr Martin also describes how when the Pope met Mikhail Gorbachev on 1st December 1989: 'At 11:03 am, he ushered Gorbachev into the library, motions him to a chair, sits down opposite him, opens his notes and starts talking. A reproduction of Poland's national treasure, the icon of Czestochowa (the Black Virgin of Jasna Gora) bearing the slash mark of a Tartar sabre on the cheek, has been placed on an easel to the right of the two leaders and some few feet from the table at which they sit.'

Paul II's 1978 election; 'no-one capable of coherent thought will easily believe that a Cardinal from behind the Iron Curtain can be anything but a Communist plant.' If *Didasco* is right, then Wojtyla deserves to go down as history's most successful double agent, having played the leading role in turning the tables on those who assured his election. The Roman Church's College of Cardinals has always been notorious for its intrigue. It may have outdone itself in the succession to John Paul I whose untimely death occurred on 28th September 1978.

In fact Tadeusz Mazowiecki was probably the Vatican's preferred choice for the Presidency. As Poland's first non-Communist prime-minister, he had demonstrated the new political realities after taking office, by going to the Vatican, rather than to Moscow . As a leader of Solidarity, he helped Walesa and others successfully to invest the Vatican's near £100 million in providing what Vatican sources have described to reporters of the Banco Ambrosiano fraud trial as 'the trip-wire for the freedom of Europe.' The less colourful Mazowiecki, another old friend of Pope John Paul, and former editor of a leading Catholic journal, was probably seen by Rome as likely to prove more reliable than Walesa in the top job. The new electorate did not agree. In the Presidential election, after it was clear that Mazowiecki was out of the running, it was reported that the Roman Catholic Church belatedly announced its support for Walesa, and Primate Cardinal Glemp cast his very influential vote for him in order to point the way to preventing the possibility of a surprise Tyminski victory.

Nevertheless Lech Walesa knows how much he owes to the Vatican and to the Pope. In February 1991, the new Polish President Walesa returned to the Vatican for his third visit there. The Roman Catholic *Universe* reported that, brimming with self-confidence he swept in to tell the Pope, 'I offer you our new Poland.' (*The Universe*: 10th February, 1991)

The new freedom experienced in Poland may not last long. There is already considerable widespread concern about the mixing of Church and State. In an article headed 'Worries over a Resurgence of Polish Catholicism', *Newsweek* magazine signalled the danger:

'The resumption of religious education in Poland's public schools is only one sign of the growing power of the church in a country that is more than ninety percent Roman Catholic. After years of wrestling with a hostile regime, the church has been embraced by Poland's new rulers, blurring the boundaries between church and state. Prime Minister Tadeusz Mazowiecki and Solidarity leader Lech Walesa regularly appear at church ceremonies; religious programmes are featured on state TV; soldiers march in a pilgrimage to the shrine of the Black Madonna, and an anti-abortion legislation dominates parliamentary deliberations. All this has prompted some Poles to wonder whether the church is not over-playing its hand. ... The decision on religious instruction has already prompted angry exchanges. Critics charge that pupils will feel pressured to enroll and that few schools provide alternative activities for those who opt not to. 'This is going from one form of indoctrination to another,' says Iwona Osuch, whose 14-year-old son sits out in the corridor while the rest of his class has religious instruction. Cardinal Jozef Glemp, the Polish primate, has blamed the scattered protests of a "very noisy minority" on the legacy of the communist system, which encouraged "an aversion to God"'. (*Newsweek*, 15th October, 1990).

In May 1991, just seven months after the *Newsweek* feature, another article called 'More Power to the Pulpit' appeared in rival magazine *Time*, confirming the swift trend towards the Church's dominance in Poland. An excerpt is quoted here:

'... When the struggle ended with a Solidarity-led government, the church emerged triumphant, firmly allied to an administration it had all but installed. A year later, the church, to which 97% of Poland's 38 million people belong, is omnipresent and, in the view of some, virtually omnipotent. Bishops and priests bless the armed forces, schools and factories. The newly created post of senior chaplain to the army has been given the rank of general. The nightly news on state-owned television unfailingly includes a church-related piece of one kind or another. On Constitution Day earlier this month, marking the 200th anniversary of Poland's first liberal constitution, President Lech Walesa, a devoted Catholic, skipped ceremonies at Parliament and instead visited the national shrine of the Black Madonna of Jasna Gora ... A poll released last week shows that the church is perceived as the single most powerful national institution, stronger than the government, the presidency, the military, the old communist *nomenklatura* and even Solidarity. The church's ascendancy has left many Poles uneasy, pondering the specter of a clerical state governed according to the dicta of Pope John Paul II, who will make his fourth visit to his native Poland in June' (*Time* magazine: May 20, 1991).

The fear that one form of intolerance has been succeeded by another was expressed by English Protestant evangelist, Roger Carswell, in the September 1989 edition of *Evangelism Today*:

'The believers in Poland have a great fear of Solidarity feeling that it will bring restrictions on evangelistic work. One of the declared aims of Solidarity is the outlawing of all religion other than Catholicism. We must pray for Poland.'

Czechoslovakia

Protestant leaders in Czechoslovakia expressed similar concerns, believing that the Roman Church had been controlling and manipulating the political situation there just as in Poland. In April 1990, Czechoslovakia became the first Warsaw Pact country visited by the Pope outside his native Poland. Just a few months before, Cardinal Tomasek, the country's Roman Catholic Primate had led 200,000 protestors calling for the end of Communist rule. He ringingly denounced the Marxist regime and called for its rulers to be punished. *The Observer* suggested that the Pope's arrival had political significance, as 'with elections only six weeks away, and with Catholic political parties among the best organised of the 27-odd in the running, the Pope's charisma will give, some charge, unfair promotion to the public image of the clerical campaigners' (*The Observer*, 22nd April, 1990).

Eugen Milo of the Slovak Reformed Church, Dr Jaroslav Ondra of the Evangelical Church of Czech Brethren and Eva Mikulecks of the Hussite Church, on a visit to Britain, in 1991, spoke of their concern about the ambitions of the Vatican: 'The Roman Church was very well prepared for the new situation, with a comprehensive plan for the "reChristianization" of Czechoslovakia. The aim is a "Christian republic", which means a Roman Catholic republic. Catholic leaders are pushing hard to equate Catholicism with nationalism and have urged "all Christians" to support the pro-Catholic *Christian Democratic Movement*.'[3] The August 1990 edition of *Christian News World* reported that with the break-up of the Communist trade unions, the Roman Catholic Church is the biggest organisation in Czechoslovakia. Slovakia, which is 90% Roman Catholic, was an independent clerical pro-Nazi State during the Second World War and is once again experiencing 'strong nationalistic feeling within the Roman Catholic Church' (*Christian News World*: August 1990).

These nationalistic feelings have led swiftly to the separation of the Slovak Republic from the Czech Republic, which took place on January 1st, 1993.

---

[3] The first political organisation to emerge in Albania in 1990 was the Christian Democratic Party.

Chapter 7

Towards Unity

The Pope has been able to carry his theme of unity into any forum however political. There were those at Strasbourg on 11th October 1988, apart from Northern Ireland Protestant leader, Revd Ian Paisley, who were asking why the Pope, who is seen as a spiritual leader, was addressing the European Parliament on **political** unity. His theme was of a united Europe, East and West, from the Urals to the Atlantic. Little more than a year afterwards his prediction seemed to be well on the way to fulfilment. Many Catholics, as well as others increasingly drawn to the Papacy, believe that the Pope had spoken prophetically. Vatican watchers are sure that the Roman Catholic institution played a major role in shaping events.

At the same time there is no doubt at all that under the Papacy of the Polish Pontiff the Catholic Church in Eastern Europe has been greatly strengthened, particularly in Poland, Czechoslovakia and Hungary.

In December 1988, Cardinal Meisner, Bishop of Berlin, an East German born in Poland, was secretly elected Archbishop of Cologne and primate of West Germany. He was the Pope's emphatic choice for the job. This may now be seen as having been a significant step towards the reunification of Germany.

The Vatican and the Kremlin

Rome formed her working alliance with the Kremlin under the pontificates of John XXIII and Paul VI in the '60s and

'70s. The new relationship was cemented by the appointment of the first East European Pope in 1978. What was started by Popes John and Paul was to continue under John Paul. The new era of 'glasnost' brought Moscow and the Vatican even closer. A very high-powered delegation of Cardinals and Vatican officials attended the Orthodox Church Millennium celebrations in Russia in 1988 and the two meetings between John Paul II and President Gorbachev followed in December 1989 and November 1990 both in the Vatican.

As we have discussed in the chapter on the Virgin Mary, the Pope has a special burden for Russia, which according to new Roman Catholic tradition: 'Our Lady of Fatima has demanded be consecrated to her immaculate heart,' with the promise that Russia 'will be converted, if my demands are listened to.'[1] According to the *Fatima* magazine, Sister Lucia, one of the three Fatima children, who is still alive, asked Jesus why He would not convert Russia without the Holy Father and the bishops making that Consecration? Jesus replied: 'Because I want My whole Church to acknowledge that Consecration as a triumph of the Immaculate Heart of Mary so that it may extend its cult (*sic*) later on and put devotion to the Immaculate Heart beside devotion to My Sacred Heart.' (*Fatima Crusader*: May, 1990)

This devotion to her immaculate heart is also 'a requisite for world peace.' Malachi Martin, former Jesuit Professor at the Vatican's Pontifical Biblical Institute, and for many years a close associate of Cardinal Bea, relates that Pope John Paul II realized, after 'exhaustive examination' of the documents, witnesses and events of Fatima, and after 'nothing less than a personal communication from Heaven,' that Fatima signified 'a geopolitical agenda attached to an

---

[1] The present Pope's predecessor, Pius XII, speaking to Portugal in October 1941, while the Nazi army rolled towards Moscow, urged Catholics to pray for the speedy realisation of Our Lady of Fatima's promises. After a speech by Hitler in 1942, claiming that Soviet Russia had definitely been defeated, Pope Pius XII in a Jubilee message over the radio, 'consecrated the whole world to the immaculate heart of Mary.' (*Vatican Imperialism in the Twentieth Century*: Avro Manhattan)

immediate timetable. Heaven's 'millennium endgame has been revealed, with John Paul as the Servant of the Grand Design.' (Malachi Martin: *The Keys of This Blood*: Simon and Schuster, New York, 1990)

Interviewed on *Denver's KLTT – 800 Radio*, Dr Martin spoke of three forces battling for total domination of the planet, as the world races toward annihilation. The contenders were John Paul II, Mikhail Gorbachev and the capitalist West. The victor, Dr Martin asserted, would be John Paul. As the world's spiritual and moral leader, he would lead a world government with absolute authority to decide all basic issues of human survival and human prosperity. What is more, he would achieve victory through the grace and power of Mary, not through Jesus Christ.

Islam and Rome

The political power wielded by the Mullahs in countries such as the former Soviet Republics and Iran that are strategic to world peace is formidable, and the Vatican is responding accordingly. Fatima and Mary, with their appeal to both Moslems and Catholics, and the wider ecumenism of the Roman Church are helping to provide the answer.

The upheavals in the Muslim world during the past few years which have brought deep disillusionment to many Muslims and many thousands of them to Christ, have also led to an increasing openness to the ecumenical movement. For example, Zaki Badawi, principal of the Muslim College of London speaking in August 1990 about Sun Myung Moon, also known as Revd Moon of the 'Moonies', acknowledged that: 'We respect his vision of bringing the world's religions together.'

The Vatican Secretariat for Non-Christians sent a message to Moslems to mark the end of the Muslim fast of Ramadan, which finished on 17th May, 1988; 'During the month of Ramadan you have shown your faith in God and your submission to his holy will. This faith in the one God, living and true, a faith which is the heritage of all the spiritual children of Abraham, the father of believers, unites us as brothers and sisters in God and encourages us to work together for solidarity, justice and peace among all peoples.' (Cardinal Arinze, *Vatican Secretariat*, May 1988)

An illustration of the practical out-working of this wider ecumenism of the Roman Church comes out of the Pope's visit to Malawi in May 1989. Arab missionaries supported by funds from oil-rich Gulf states were at that time increasingly active in that central African nation. Reacting to the problems caused by this to the Mother Church, the Pope said: 'What is required is mutual respect, as well as mutual recognition of those things we share in common.' Then in a prayer service attended by 15 representatives of different faiths, including a Muslim leader, the Pope declared that the Church wished to pursue a 'dialogue of heart and mind' with all religions and work together with them to build up Malawi. The Church of Rome is very serious about inter-faith ecumenism.

Another example to illustrate just how seriously the Papacy is pursuing the new strategy comes from Rome itself. There, the Vatican's mass-media company, *St Paul Audiovisuals*, is producing a 26-part cartoon version of the Koran for Arab TV. The work which will take three years and cost £15 million is in partnership with the *International Islamic Society*.

'We are co-producing in the interests of ecumenism,' said Fr Eligio Ermeti of St Paul's, who admitted that problems abounded; not least presumably, that the Koran condemns as infidels those who believe that God has a son. (*Catholic Herald*: 7 July 1989)

The Roman Empire Restored

Apart from the re-emergence of militant Islam, the alliance of Marxism and Catholicism was the remarkable phenomenon of the thirty years to the end of the 80s. This unlikely partnership brought together religion and revolution, and a strengthening of the Roman Church as economic failure weakened the Communist grip. Many evangelical Christians, believing that we are nearing 'the end of the end time', are still convinced, in spite of what has happened in Eastern Europe, that the joining together of the two great world systems of Socialism and Catholicism is the unholy alliance of the beast and the false prophet of the book of *Revelation 16:13 & 19:20*.

A carefully laid clue to what was happening at the end of the last decade may have been provided by the December 1988 edition of *The Economist*, under the heading 'A Common Market for the Spirit': 'Two ideas inveigled Europe in 1988: the EEC's single European market and Mikhail Gorbachev's misty talk of a 'common European home.' Watch out, says our special correspondent in Vatican City, for the coming of a third Euro-idea in 1989: the Pope's.'

Newsweek magazine described the Euro-idea in a September 1987 article; 'The Pope's international design is a Utopian vision of a unified and Christianized Europe stretching from the Atlantic ocean to the Ural mountains.' Pope John Paul has announced a Europe-wide meeting of Bishops in 1991 to draft a strategy designed to meet his vision for a kind of Golden Age of Christian Europe, prompting the *European* newspaper to observe: 'There is growing evidence that the Vatican's diplomatic advances are also giving the Church a leading role in the political reform of Eastern Europe.'

The revelations in *Time* magazine in February, 1992, uncovered by Watergate reporter Carl Bernstein, relating to the Vatican's role in Poland, and wider role in the defeat of Communism, certainly confirms this.[2] The Papacy no longer merely proposes, once again she disposes.

Many believe, and not only Christians, that Europe is destined to be the centre of a final world empire, as the Holy Roman Empire restored. *The European* newspaper reported in November 1990 that; 'the Christian Democratic leaders from Belgium, Germany, Greece, Italy, Luxemberg and the Netherlands backed far-reaching plans for transfer of national sovereignty and the establishment of a federal government, with sole control over monetary, foreign and defence policy.' Just a week after this

---

[2] See 'Prologue' at the front of this book.

announcement by the European Heads of Government, Margaret Thatcher, who had so resolutely opposed the advance of federalism, was removed from power.

All the political change that has so swiftly taken place, the apparent collapse of the Soviet empire, the emergence of democracy in Eastern Europe, and the forming of the unprecedented United Nations coalition for the Gulf War, even allying Muslims with the West against Muslims, suggests that union, both political and spiritual, may not be far off. The Bible certainly predicts this ultimate confederacy, as well as comprehensively warning us about it.

European Union

Our country's Protestant, Reformed and Biblical heritage has guided us as a nation away from organic ties of any kind with Roman Catholic States. British foreign policy for centuries was wary of unity and always aimed at maintaining the balance of power in Europe. Prior to the fateful signing of the **Treaty of Rome**, the whole thrust of policy, Empire and Commonwealth, had been directed in opposition to any kind of European integration. Margaret Thatcher, unlike her immediate predecessors as Prime Minister, was squarely in this tradition, jealous of British greatness and deeply opposed to European federalism and wary of the intentions of the Eurocrats in Brussels. Her differences with Jacques Delors, President of the European Commission and architect of the growing European Super State, were visceral.

Roman Catholic *Sunday Telegraph* Editor, Peregrine Worsthorne described Jacques Delors as 'from a strongly Catholic French family,' who 'has a brand of Social Catholicism which is hostile to the individualistic capitalism of the English-speaking world.' (*Sunday Telegraph*, 6th January, 1991) For Monsieur Delors, who addressed the Plenary Assembly of French Catholic Bishops at Lourdes in October 1989, Socialism runs second to Catholicism.

Jacques Delors is a product of a Catholic social movement, as are German Chancellor Helmut Kohl, former President Andreotti of Italy, Prime Minister Felipe

Gonzales of Spain and former Prime Minister Tadeusz Mazowiecki of Poland. The Catholic Social Movement believes that 'there is no nobler task than the unifying of our continent.'[3]

Dutch Prime Minister, Rund Lubbers, a devout Catholic who attended a Jesuit College, was the architect of the Maastrict Treaty on Political Union (*Catholic Herald*, 13th November, 1992). Lubbers has worked closely with fellow federalist Jacques Delors, also Jesuit-educated, in furthering the Maastrict agenda, undeterred by the mounting distrust of the Treaty of the people of Europe. In Britain, in spite of the opt-out clauses that tempted us in, and the provision of 'subsidiarity', the political establishment has been split.

Subsidiarity is a thoroughly Jesuitical concept, capable of meaning many things to many people. There is no definition of it in the draft of the Maastrict Treaty. It will mean what people wish it to mean, presumably principally those at the centre of power. The fact that it hasn't been flatly rejected unhappily reflects on the indecisiveness and lack of statesmanship of the government.

The Daily Telegraph's Peterborough column reported on 14th October, 1989 that the then Chancellor, John Major, amidst fears of Britain being by-passed over future monetary strategy, claimed to be setting the European agenda. 'He made much play with 'subsidiarity.' I wrongly thought that this clumsy word was another bit of new-minted Eurojargon, but a Catholic friend tells me that it is in fact established Vaticanspeak and first cropped up in Pius XI's 1931 Encyclical, *Quadragesimo Anno* – an origin which may only inflame the suspicions of those who believe that the Community is simply the Holy Roman Empire revisited.'

Peregrine Worsthorne arrived at the same conclusion. Writing in August, 1991, in another leading article in the *Sunday Telegraph*, headed 'Now a Holy Roman Empire?',

---

[3] The first EEC Ambassador to the United States was described by Sky TV's 'Hour of Power' programme in February 1993 as 'a Dutch, devoted Roman Catholic'.

Worsthorne described John Paul II as 'the most political Pope of modern times.' 'It is in the movement towards federalism of the Common Market, with the coming membership of East European countries, as well as in the turmoil of the Soviet Union, that the Pope may see the greatest possibility for an increase in Catholic political power since the fall of Napoleon, or since the Counter-Reformation. ... If European federalism triumphs, the EC will indeed be an empire. It will lack an emperor; but it will have the Pope. It is difficult not to think that Wojtyla realises this.'

The Papacy may succeed in doing more than reviving the old Holy Roman Empire. As Professor Malachi Martin reasons, 'The Papacy is best placed to run any world government which may emerge.' 'If tomorrow or next week by a sudden miracle, a one-world government were established, the Roman Church stands alone ... as the first fully realised, fully practising and totally independent geopolitical force in the current world arena. And the Pope is by definition the world's first fully fledged geopolitical leader.'

Chapter eleven of the book of Genesis describes Babel, where mankind was unified politically and linguistically. The people began to build a tower for themselves to reach Heaven. God scattered them and separated the languages to confound both unity and rebellion. There could be no unity under Him for a fallen world. The unity that would be obtained was that of *the god of this world, who has blinded the eyes of those who do not believe* (2 Corinthians 4:4); or Satan, also described in the Bible as the Devil. Babel became the Babylon that runs like a thread through the Bible, caused the captivity of God's people Israel and then as 'mystery Babylon', which has caused the peoples of the world to worship a false politico-religious, and now economic, Beast system, until its fall.

> *'For God hath put in their hearts to fulfil his will, and to agree, and to give their kingdom unto the beast, until the words of God shall be fulfilled.'*   Revelation 17:17

Signs of the Times

Under a picture of the Tower of Babel, a Council of Europe advertisement depicts Europe: 'Many tongues, one voice.' Many Christians see the European Community, rapidly developing into a United States of Europe, as a fulfillment of biblical prophecy as well as a revival of a kind of Holy Roman Empire.

The British Post Office produced a special stamp for the 1984 European Elections which displayed a picture of a loosely clad woman, resembling a harlot riding on a beast like a bull. Europe's flag has a circle of twelve stars and is coloured blue, a configuration and colour very closely resembling countless Catholic pictures of the The Virgin Mary. A similar depiction, this time of the European political confederacy appeared in *Time* Magazine in December, 1991. *Time* explained that they had based the picture on Homer's *Iliad*, showing Europa, the daughter of Phoenix, scantily dressed, riding on Zeus in the form of a bull.

The Gibraltar twenty pence coin, closely resembling the one in circulation in Britain, has a Madonna and Child image ringed by the words 'Our Lady of Europa'.

The future coinage intended for a United Europe is the Ecu, described by *The Sunday Telegraph* as 'the Ecumenical coin'. Three of four coins, minted in Belgium, have the image of historical heads of Europe, united as the Holy Roman Empire, namely Charlemagne, Charles V and the eighteenth century Hapsburg Empress Maria Theresa. The fourth coin, the 25 Ecu piece, is of the Roman Emperor Diocletian who attempted to restore the old pagan form of religion by the severe persecution of Christians at the beginning of the fourth century.

A well-orchestrated publicity drive has pushed the Hapsburg family back into the limelight in Austrian political circles. The last Crown Prince, Otto, a Euro MP for the right-wing Christian Social Union in his adopted Bavaria, is convinced that the day of a European 'Reich' will dawn. The campaign to annul the so-called Hapsburg laws (barring the revival of the Empire) has the support of a large circulation newspaper and many conservative politicians. Otto and his son, Karl, are both working for the family's ideals – transnational ideals – in a modern political form (*Sunday Telegraph*, 22nd November, 1992).[4]

The Protestant Alliance has asked 'why nobody informed us that the stars on the "European Flag" are meant to symbolise the new "Holy Roman Empire", with Mary symbolised as the "Queen of Europe". With the European Commission going on a pilgrimage to Rome, and other Brussels delegates travelling to Santiago de Compostela just to mark a jubilee of "Europe". . . Facts like these should have been told to the people' (*The Reformer*, January/February, 1993).

---

[4] Together with two other Roman Catholics, Dr Otto was a member of The Committee for *ProChrist 93*, Billy Graham's campaign in Essen, Germany, in March 1993.

Chapter 8

Multi-Faith and the New Age

Meanwhile ecclesiastically the Pope reigns supreme. On the world stage, successive Archbishops of Canterbury have deferred naturally to him. Illustrative of this was the *Daily Telegraph* headline: 'A pipe of peace at Pope's prayer day', referring to the 27th October, 1986 Assisi *World Day of Prayer*, when the warring factions in Nicaragua, El Salvador and elsewhere laid down their arms, involved amongst others Archbishop Runcie, the Dalai Lama, Hindus, Sikhs, Muslims, Bahais, Shintoists and pagan cult leaders, even including snake worshippers from Togo. *(world Council of Churches)*

Although the Roman Catholic church is not officially one of the 317 member churches of the WCC, about 25 per cent of WCC staff are Roman Catholics.

Rome's leadership of both the peace movement, and the multi-faith advance towards religious unity, parallels her central role in the quest for political unity. Multi-faith religion can now readily be seen as closely associated with the Church of Rome through the many initiatives taken by the Vatican. Assisi was the venue which readily commended itself to the *World Wide Fund for Nature's* President, the Duke of Edinburgh, to stage that organisation's 25th Anniversary special event. The shrine of St Francis, the increasingly important patron Saint of animals (and their conservation), played a significant role in that event. In fact two separate events, the meeting of the religious leaders and the WWF anniversary took place consecutively, so that many people had the opportunity to attend and influence both.

Following on from that trail-blazing initiative of combining world faiths there has been a succession of inter-faith festivals and services organised in Britain's leading Cathedrals by New Ager Martin Palmer and others. The first at Winchester in 1987, which was a *Creation Harvest Festival* launching the *Rainbow Covenant* between man and nature, was followed by conferences and festivals linking faith and ecology, at Coventry, Birmingham, Canterbury and Salisbury Cathedrals. The Canterbury gathering in September 1989 enabled three separate pilgrimages to converge at the site where King Henry II submitted to the Pope. After this the combined procession led by the Archbishop of York, a leading ecumenist, made its way to pray at Thomas a Becket's shrine inside the Cathedral. Thus it was that at Canterbury in September 1989, at this *Conference on Christian Faith and Ecology*, inter-faith and ecumenical religion were seen and experienced together as one.

'Green' issues, so important now politically, have been important to the Vatican from before the beginnings of ecological concern in the 1960s, and have been linked to the Roman Church's leadership of the wider peace movement, The theme for the *World Day of Peace* in 1990 was 'peace with God the Creator, peace with all of creation'. The Vatican statement, announcing the Day of Peace, spoke of ecological problems reflecting a 'moral crisis' in understanding the relationship between human beings and the environment.

The five world faiths that signed the Declarations at Assisi had become seven when they addressed both Houses of Parliament in 1988. As at Assisi, a Franciscan, this time a Friar, spoke for Christianity. In May 1989, at the United Nations Building in New York, the Duke of Edinburgh launched the *International Sacred Literature Trust*, which he believes 'will make a significant contribution to inter-faith dialogue.'

A comment from Dave Hunt, evangelical commentator and author of *The Seduction of Christianity* helps us to see a clearer picture:

'The current Pope is the leader of worldwide ecumenism. As such he presents an altogether different picture from the inflexible dogmatist determined to convert the world to Catholicism that most people imagine a pope to personify. On the contrary, John Paul II has taken the initiative in contacting leaders of the world's religions, accepts them as working towards the same goals of social justice, ecological wholeness and world peace, suggests that their prayers are as effective as those of Catholics, and has not attempted to convert any of them. He seems content to be acknowledged as the spiritual leader of the world's religions uniting for peace.'

Yet at the same time, this same Pope continues to claim that the Roman Church is the bride of Christ, the one true church devoted to one person, the Son of the living God. What is described in this section is not the behaviour of a bride, chaste and pure; it is the behaviour of an harlot, readily recognisable as the *great whore* of *Revelation 17.*

Christians were encouraged by the appointment of a declared evangelical at the See of Canterbury, and one who at his enthronement appeared to be affirming the unique standing of the Christian gospel among world religions. Addressing leaders of other faiths assembled in Canterbury Cathedral, George Carey said: 'The faith that I have in Christ and in His good news is so important that I am compelled; necessity is layed upon me, to share it with all people. But I trust that I can listen to your story and respect your integrity, even though, I may still want to offer you, as to all, the claims of my Lord.'

However, in office, George Carey has adopted a totally different position. He has taken issue with the 2000 evangelical clergymen who petitioned Her Majesty the Queen in protest over the Commonwealth Interfaith Service at Westminster Abbey. Speaking in September, 1992, at a session of the Conference of European Churches in Prague, he said: 'We dare not allow our peoples to return to historic rivalries. In this context not only ecumenism but also interfaith co-operation is paramount.'

Long regarded by conservative evangelicals as 'wobbly', the Archbishop is already appearing to seek to be all things to all men. Certainly his support of the *Evangelical Catholic Alliance* in Northern Ireland, which aims to prove it possible to be both Evangelical and Roman Catholic at the same time, bears this out.

The New Age

Vatican II's *Nostra Aetate* included this statement; 'Different religions have tried to respond to mankind's search for the ultimate explanation of creation and the meaning of man's journey through life. The Catholic church accepts the truth and goodness found in these religions and she sees reflections there of the Truth of Christ, whom she proclaims as 'the Way, the Truth and the Life.' She wishes to do everything possible to cooperate with other believers in preserving all that is good in their religions and cultures.'

The omnipresent New Age movement which came into the open in 1975 is also helping to bring the world religions together, especially through Western adoption of aspects of Hindu and Buddhist thought and practice. The Roman Catholic Church has done much to contribute to this in advancing its strategy for ecumenical and religious co-operation. For example, the entire May/June edition of *The Catholic World*, in 1990, was given over to Buddhism. Among the articles included in that edition were 'The Buddha Revered as a Christian Saint' and a glowing biography of 'His Holiness the Dalai Lama.' The Tibetan Buddhist was described as having frequent contact with Catholic leaders, including 'his old friend', John Paul II, whom he has met at least five times and Paul VI, with whom he had two meetings. The present Pope has endorsed him as 'a great spiritual leader'. Like Mother Teresa and Lech Walesa, the Dalai Lama is also a Nobel Peace prize-winner. At his initiation ceremony he was named; 'the holy one, the tender glory, mighty in speech, of excellent intellect, of absolute wisdom, holding the doctrine, the ocean.' (*Chambers Encyclopedia*: Volume 13, p 621)

It is instructive, as we consider these things, to remember

that at the *First Parliament of World Religions* Conference at Chicago in 1892 the objective stated by widely acclaimed Eastern mystic, Swami Vivekananda was to be 'a society compounded of Western Science, Socialism and Indian Spirituality.' *The Second Parliament of World Religions*, which took place in 1992 at the *Temple of Understanding*, 'the Spiritual United Nations', in Washington DC, was able to celebrate the near fulfillment of Vivekananda's prophecy.

In 1981 the Pope spoke of the special place Rome accords to Eastern religions. 'Ways must be discovered,' he said, 'to make the dialogue with all religions become a reality everywhere, but especially in Asia, the cradle of ancient cultures and religions.' Just nine years later he predicted that a new injection of life for the Church in the next few years would come from the East. Just as worshippers do in Roman Catholic ritual, the Pope is looking towards the East. Flying over Moscow, (something permitted to the Papacy for the first time in more than 85 years), on his way to Seoul, the Pope is said to have exclaimed: 'Lux ex Oriente. There will be new religious life in Europe from the East.'

Ecumenism, Mysticism and the New Age

Annie Besant, pioneer theosophist, in her book, *Mysticism*, wrote;

> '... The Roman Catholic has always kept a knowledge of that Path and method by which the supreme knowledge may be gained. He calls the end of it by a startling name. Generally the word Union is used, but take up some great book of Roman Catholic theology and you will find the startling word which I have in mind; they call it Deification, the deification of man, man become God, for nothing less than that is meant by Deification. And the Hindu and the Buddhist call it Liberation, the setting free of the human Spirit from the bonds which have tied him down, from the matter which has blinded him. The meaning is the same, the method is the same, the thing the same. And so we realise that in the realm of the Spirit there are none of those divisions that mark

off one religion from another in the separative plane of earth, and we realise that the Spirit is united where earth holds diversity, and that where knowledge takes the place of faith, there controversies sink into silence and the certainty of truth is known.' (Annie Besant: *Mysticism*: Theosophical Publishing Society, 1914).

There is much in Roman Catholic tradition to contribute to New Age thinking; mysticism, medieval and modern; the writings and activities of prominent Catholics, past and present, such as Teilhard de Chardin, Thomas Merton, Matthew Fox and Mother Teresa; the output of educational institutions such as the Jesuit Georgetown University in Washington DC, including that of leading conspiracy theorist, Georgetown Professor Carol Quigley.

Teilhard, also a Jesuit professor, sowed many seeds for the New Age Movement, especially in relation to man's control over the evolutionary process. Fr Thomas Merton championed the merger of Zen Buddhism and Christianity. American Dominican Matthew Fox's 'Creation-centred Spirituality', based on multi-faith and pagan ideas is bringing 'deep ecumenism' and 'deep ecology' together within the New Age. Mother Teresa has made a major contribution to the new universal religion. In 1981, at St James' Church, Piccadilly, London, which through its rector Donald Reeves, has a growing relationship with New Age centre Findhorn, in Invernesshire, Mother Teresa gave the first public pronouncement of Satish Kumer's Hindu 'Universal Prayer for Peace,' now widely used by ecumenical churches. Mother Teresa has been an honorary guest at 'intercultural, inter-faith gatherings' in Malta and in Oxford.

The Malta Conference, in March 1985, organised 'to celebrate 40 years United Nations,' brought together representatives of religious groupings, including shamanism, kabbalism, occultism, the peace movement and the ecumenical movement. Among those attending were New Age leaders including author Marilyn Ferguson and UN Assistant Secretary General Robert Muller, as well as the Dalai

*Mother Teresa of Calcutta addressing a prayer for peace meeting
at St. James's church in London's Piccadilly.*
© The Press Association, July 1981

Lama. The Dalai Lama himself presides over a religion
which incorporates strands of Mahayana Buddhism, mixed
with the mystical formularies, magic and occult of the Tan-
trayana and Tibetan Shamanism, which is also based on
magic and sorcery. (Alan Morrison: *The Trojan Horse in the
Temple*, *The Bulwark*, Sept/Oct 1989)

Ecumenism and the New Age

The ecumenical link with the 'new age' movement is very apparent. In her book, The Findhorn Community, Carol Riddell, resident at Findhorn, sociologist and devotee of Indian yogi Sai Baba, states that, 'Sufism, Transcendental Meditation and the entire Christian ecumenical movement, exemplified by the Taize community, are our brothers and sisters in the network of light.' (Carol Riddell: *The Findhorn Community*, Findhorn Press)

'Part of the Aquarian Age is the rediscovery of feminine goddess energy, as opposed to the patriarchal aggressively male energy of the last 2000 years', claimed one of many positive feature articles about the New Age now appearing in the press. (*Sunday Telegraph*: 28 April 1991). *Time* magazine reported in May 1991 that Mother Earth worship services are part of 'a growing United States spiritual movement, Goddess worship, the effort to create a female-centered focus for spiritual expression ... Adherents claim that the movement involves as many as 100,000 US women. Though such ancient goddesses as Isis and Astarte are often invoked, most worship occurs in the name of a vague generic "Goddess", often depicted as Mother Earth or Gaia in line with enviromental awareness.' (*Time* magazine: May 6, 1991) The historical roots of the rapidly expanding cult of Mary with the worship of ancient goddesses and other pagan practices have been examined in an earlier chapter; such links seem sure to strengthen.

The New Age Movement is undoubtedly advancing on many fronts, not least in the Church which 'will not endure sound doctrine ... having itching ears'. Many Christians have drunk deep drafts of New Age potions; for example, holistic health, hypnosis, yoga, inner healing, meditation, psychical research and awareness training; and many have imbibed new doctrines and heresies, based on the humanistic and 'positive' thinking of Teilhard, Norman Vincent Peale and others, which provide the Church with its emphasis on an earthly kingdom now, the social gospel and society reconstructed or Christianized, with 'kingdom principles', for the Lord's return.

Restorationist leader, Bryn Jones, writing at the beginning of 1991, promised his followers that; 'By the power of his Spirit we will bring all that is against God and man beneath Christ's authority. God's Church will be the most influential body of people on earth in the final period of this age.' This is indeed a prophetic word, but it is fulfilled in Scripture only by the Apostate Church of the Book of Revelation.

John Gimenez, National Chairman of *Washington for Jesus* in 1988, told that gathering of 500,000 people, from 17 Christian denominations; 'We believe that it is God's will that the righteous should reign on this earth, and we're seeing people preparing themselves to be lawyers, doctors, generals, admirals, presidents and congressmen. The righteous shall rule and the people will rejoice.'

One of the righteous he probably had in mind was Pat Robertson, who had run for the Presidency of the United States that year. Mr Robertson, head of the prestigious Christian Broadcasting Network and leader of the 'religious right' in the United States, wrote in his 1982 book *The Secret Kingdom*; 'It is clear that God is saying, "I gave man dominion over the earth but he lost it. Now I desire mature sons and daughters who will in My name exercise dominion over the earth and will subdue Satan, the unruly and the rebellious. Take back my world from those who would use it and abuse it. Rule as I would rule."'

This statement of a very powerful and influential leader of American Christians is a chilling indication of how closely parallelled are the names and pronouncements of ecumenical Christianity and the New Age Movement. It might very well have been said by a New Ager, seeking the 'new order' of dominion and peace and looking to 'little gods' who will emerge in the *Age of Aquarius*, acting for God in judgment and subduing Satan, including those who dissent.

The church does not have a mandate in the Bible to set up the Kingdom for God, although Restorationists with their 'apostles' and 'prophets', Reconstructionists, Latter-Rain, Kingdom Now, Manifest Sons of God, Dominionists, followers of Word of Faith, Positive Confession and Prosperity schools, and advocates of the 'Social Gospel', all have the church restoring the kingdom of Christ for His coming.

Before his scourging, Jesus told Pilate: 'My kingdom is not

of this world; if my kingdom were of this world, then would my servants fight.'

ΕΚΚΛΗΘΙΑ

The great commission is the assignment of the church to call believers out of the kingdoms of this world, not to take back the kingdoms of this world for Christ.

Smokescreen

New Age Observer and author, Roy Livesey, is convinced that much of what we see is an elaborately devised smoke-screen for the deception fashioned by the Jesuit Order and the Church of Rome. For example Mr Livesey sees Professor Quigley's influential book *Tragedy and Hope*, the study of global conspiracy, as part of the subtle deception pointing away from the antichrist.[1] Mr Livesey who was converted out of the New Age movement, argues in his book *Understanding the New Age* that Quigley's conspiratorial view of history, which spawned so many others in its wake, explored every suspect avenue except that of his own Jesuit Order, historically the most likely culprit. Another Professor of History, Norman Cohn, writing about 'the myth of the Jewish World conspiracy,' states in his book *Warrant for Genocide* that it can be traced back to a French Jesuit, Abbé Barruel, who appears to have instigated the myth, on which the infamous *Protocols of Zion* were based.

The Pope is well placed to emerge as spiritual leader of the New Age movement as it set its sights, in parallel with the Decade of Evangelisation, towards 2000 AD and the beginning of the Age of Aquarius, or the Age of the Spirit.

Like the Vatican, the New Age has close links with powerful organisations such as the United Nations, UNESCO, the World Council of Churches, the Club of Rome, the Trilateral Commission, the Bilderberg Group

See A Morning me

---

[1] Let us stop to ask the simple question, who is the antichrist? The antichrist defined by Scripture is *'he who denies the Father and the Son.'* (1 John 2:18) The line of Popes has denied the Father and the Son by taking their place. The Pope of Rome has claimed throughout Christian history to represent Christ as 'Vicar of Christ' and to be 'Holy Father', known today to countless millions of the faithful as 'Papa'.

and the Freemasons. Other organisations and movements with a political agenda, such as the conservationist and the many and various peace and disarmament groups, also act as a veil behind which one-world government and one-world religion are taking shape.

As suggested earlier in this book, Mary, the Mother and Virgin Queen, has near universal appeal. She is already playing a major role in helping to bring together a one-world religion, and is certainly attracting New Age devotees too. She is readily associated with Mother Earth, the creation from man's perspective and the pagan Earth goddess Gaia. Her apparitions at Medjugorje since 1981 are supported by Benjamin Creme's Tara Centre as a 'sign' that 'Maitreya, the Christ' is in the world, according to New Age author Elizabeth Clare Prophet, writing about *Mother Mary's New Age Teaching and Rosary*. (Elizabeth C. and Mark L. Prophet: Summit University Press, 1974)

Chapter 9

Protestantism Under Siege

As a member of the London-based United Protestant Council put it; 'As it is Protestantism which stands in the way of a united Papal Ireland, so it is Protestantism, its resistance decreasing rapidly, but still exercising the power of prayer, which prevents the domination of the Roman system everywhere else.' The author of this book recognizes that the term Protestant is problematic for many because of its association with the excesses and extremes of behaviour that are reported in the press relating to Northern Ireland. Although there are probably more Bible-believing Christians there in proportion to population than perhaps anywhere else, any one can adopt any label to gain respectability. As in the Lebanon, the term Christian is widely used by political parties and factions as well as military groups. The revenge-seeking terrorists totally discredit the term Protestant and are in no wise submitted to Christ and His Word. The term 'evangelical' no longer carries the meaning that it once did either, referring now to all those who take on board as much sound doctrine only as squares with their own particular world view.

Managing the Media

As the Roman 'sun' has risen, so the Protestant light has dimmed. Somehow, imperceptibly and subtly, the Protestant character of the Anglican and Non-conformist faith has been undermined in the public perception. Protestanism has

102

become a term of abuse to many, tainted as it is by the violence and rhetoric of Northern Ireland politics, but the skill with which the Roman Catholic institution, with its long practised and admired mastery over both information and 'dis-information', manages the media, is unique in the field of public relations.

As the Apostle John expressed it in Revelation 17:6, *'and when I saw her I wondered with great admiration.'* So very often the religious hero of stage, films, TV and radio is the Roman Catholic priest or nun. Not all that long ago, it was almost an event to see a nun in public; by definition they were usually hidden from view. Now we see them prominently and frequently in the media, playing snooker, employing entrepreneurial skills, standing their ground and defending their rights and what is right.

Likewise, media coverage of important events and national tragedies increasingly seem to give prominence to the Roman Catholic faith. Feature articles in the influential press, Sunday services on TV, religious programmes and plays on BBC radio, all seem to be heading in the same 'ecumenical' direction.

We may expect this trend to continue and gather pace following the recent appointment of Jesuit-educated Stephen Whittle to the post of Head of Religious Programmes, BBC TV. In an interview with the Roman Catholic newspaper *The Universe*, he spoke enthusiastically of the 'enormous impact of the Catholic Church', of the 'terrific "Songs of Praise" which came from Westminster Cathedral with Cardinal Hume' (on Easter Day). He also spoke of 'the programmes on prayer, which are being repeated, done by Fr Gerry Hughes – a Jesuit, by the way!' and of how 'for him, the Eucharist is the heart of Christianity'. (*The Universe* 23rd April, 1989)[1]

---

[1] Jesuit Fr Gerry Hughes made ecumenical history at the annual Baptist Assembly in April 1991 when he became the first Catholic priest to address a major session of the assembly. Fr Hughes SJ received an enthusiastic reception from more than one thousand Baptists meeting at Bournemouth International Centre, with his address on the Spirituality of Freedom. (*The Universe*: 5th May 1991)

Catholic Charismatics, like Charles Whitehead, Jesuit-educated international co-ordinator for Charismatic Renewal for England and Wales, are beginning to feature on TV and the other media, as the Charismatic movement becomes established. An article in *The Sunday Telegraph* in March 1991 argued that with George Carey as Archbishop of Canterbury, the Charismatic Renewal, already well on the way, is likely before long to become 'the establishment' within the established Church of England. We can thus expect religious programming on TV and radio to increasingly feature ecumenical leaders like Charles White-head and David Alton.

Christmas 1990 demonstrated the trend towards Roman Catholic Church services on TV. Four out of seven pro-grammes relating to Christianity from 24th–26th December were filmed in Roman Catholic Churches or dealt with the lives of Roman Catholic churchmen.

The Christmas edition of the *Sunday Times* magazine of 24th December, 1988 majored on the theme 'Who Was Jesus?' The front cover featured the Virgin Mary enthroned as Queen of Heaven, wearing a tiara, glittering with jewell-ery and holding a baby Jesus with flaxen hair. Inside under the heading – 'What Happened to Christianity?,' much acclaimed novelist and Catholic, Anthony Burgess, author of *A Clockwork Orange*, wrote as if Roman Catholicism were the majority and not a minority faith in this country.

Other Roman Catholics, celebrities whose claim to fame, on the face of it, would not seem to have a ready connection with their religious faith, feature prominently in articles about the Roman Catholic faith in the media. An example of this was the exposure given to the faith of the novelist, and lapsed Catholic, Graham Greene in several newspapers after his 85th birthday in 1989. The extraordinary aspect of this reporting was the evident conclusion that Mr Greene, who styled himself a 'Catholic agnostic' had very little faith, if any. Some of his novels deal with the themes of faith and guilt, reflecting the author's experiences with Catholicism, which he thought 'nearer the truth than other religions of the world', rather than his devotion to it. The Observer article quoted another national newspaper 'billing him as possibly the world's most famous Catholic layman' and comes to the conclusion at the end of the piece that 'serious is the one thing Mr Greene's Christianity is not.' (*The Observer* : 8th October, 1989) Yet when Mr Greene died in 1991, prominent in the news bulletins were descriptions of him as 'a convert to Catholicism'.

Just as the World Wide Fund for Nature chose Franciscans to represent Christianity for their inter-faith initiative, so also did the TV companies select a Roman Catholic as spokesman for Christianity during the Gulf War at the end of 1990. Their choice was devout Catholic, Brigadier Hammerbeck; but according to a report in the *Daily Telegraph*; 'in his final message to the troops, the Brigadier decided to quote from the gospel according to Star Wars rather than the Bible. "The force is with us", he told the headquarter troops of the Royal Scots. "God bless you all. We are going to do the business".' (*Daily Telegraph*: 4th February 1991)

Poet Gerald Manley Hopkins, has been featured in the media on a number of occasions, where emphasis has been placed more on his contribution to the Jesuit Order than his contribution to English verse. The 'spiritual exercises' of Ignatius Loyola, deeply alien to Bible-believing Christians, but an important aspect of the poet's Catholic faith, have been given a good deal of air-time alongside him.

Subtly and engagingly, with few people aware that it is happening, the practices of the Roman Church, including the mass, the rosary, prayers for the dead, praying to the Saints and to Mary, to idols and icons, have come more and more into use and are associated with Christianity in the minds of readers, viewers and listeners. In such a climate those who oppose such practices are out of step, unreasonable and intolerant.

Protestantism or Bible-believing Christianity does not fare nearly so well in the media. The former Moderator of the Free Church of Scotland, Angus Smith, reacted to all that is going on in forthright fashion; 'The most bigoted church in the world has smothered Protestantism with propaganda against bigotry.'

Protestant publications are not reviewed in the media, nor are their concerns and warnings given coverage, unless there is some form of dramatic public confrontation. There is concern that following the Salman Rushdie affair, revision of the blasphemy law would be used to prevent distribution of books, tapes and tracts warning of the dangers of ecumenism, interchurch and interfaith. Such a law would be a reversal of the freedoms that stem from the reformation, that flowed from the *Bill of Rights* and *Acts of Toleration* and led to the much abused *Catholic Emancipation Act*.

Scottish Reformation Society Secretary General, Sinclair Horne, speaking in 1981, claimed that 'most leading editors of our newspapers and most leading Television Producers were Roman Catholics.'

Certainly 10 years later it is still true of a very high proportion of editors, proprietors, religious correspondents and leading columnists of the press. The House of Commons press launch of *Spirit of '88*, an enterprise set up in 1988, to commemorate co-inciding major anniversaries of our Christian heritage such as the placing of the English Bible in all the churches, deliverance from the Armada and the 'Glorious Revolution', was attended by journalists from leading national newspapers, and addressed by well known churchmen. However not a word was printed. One young reporter from a leading national daily said that he was 'amazed by his editor's decision to exclude the article that he had prepared.'

In sharp contrast, as we examine later, Vatican press disclosures are printed in full and often supported editorially. Such 'disclosures' often include material contributing to the carefully orchestrated public line that the Vatican is taking on a particular issue. For example, pleading poverty to combat 'exaggerated tales' of her great wealth provides regular material for the press.

Concerning Church unity, occasional headline stories to rock the ecumenical boat have appeared during the top-level meetings and negotiations, strengthening the Vatican hand inexorably. They claim to come from 'unofficial Vatican sources', as if they had been leaked, although Vatican watchers deny that this happens. For example on Easter Day 1989 *The Mail on Sunday* in banner headlines declared 'CRISIS AS THE POPE BLAMES RUNCIE – Primate flying to Vatican to save Church unity talks.' Such impact-making press coverage undoubtably bolsters Rome's bargaining position and in the current climate strengthens her hand inexorably.

The Pope's role as the peace-maker could hardly enjoy a more favourable coverage in the media. Even when he adopts a political position deeply unpopular in the West, such as his strong criticism of the Allies' decision to go to war against Saddam Hussein, it does not seem to surface, and he escapes opprobium.

There is a Roman Catholic Training School at Hatch End in Middlesex where are located 'the best equipped TV studios possibly in the world, the purpose of which is specifically to train and prepare producers, directors, programme presenters, priests and nuns for TV broadcasting. 'In fact the Roman Catholic Church operates a guild of media personalities', according to the Protestant newspaper, the *Orange Standard*. (*Orange Standard*, March 1991). The radio and TV Centre at Hatch End has as its director Dr James McDonnell, who was previously in charge of projects at the Jesuit-run *Centre for the Study of Communication and Culture*. (*Daily Telegraph*: February 6th 1990)

Lumen 2000, the Media arm of Evangelization 2000, the Decade of Evangelization, is described by the *Catholic Herald* as a 'mammoth religious road-show with a vision of piping papal masses, messages and images to all corners of the five continents.' Lumen 2000, which began operations in Rome in 1987, had its first major broadcast with the launch of *The Marian Year* in 1987 via eighteen satellites to an audience of two billion people. (*Evangelical Times*, February 1991)

The Public Relations Campaign For *Evangelization 2000* is being run by Richard Pollen, Chief Executive of the publicity firm that he founded, *Valin Pollen*. Pollen's brief from the Vatican is to convert as many unbelievers as possible to Christianity, preferably to the Roman Catholic branch, by 25th December, AD 2000.

Catholic Action

Paralleling and complementing the public relations offensive is that which the Scottish evangelical magazine

Bulwark calls the power of *Catholic Action*. 'Someone said recently that Rome laughs when her power is discussed on a merely theological level, for she knows that her real advancement lies in the way that she can pull the strings of political power and manipulate situations to her advantage. ... Few people realise how carefully organised *Catholic Action* is, and it is only when one who has been involved in this movement, tells of its policy and methods that a true realisation of its power and scope are revealed. Every segment of our society is infiltrated by these agents, who are highly trained, paid and equipped by the Church to do this work. Perhaps its greatest work is done in the political field where its objective is to get laws passed which foster the cause of Roman Catholicism in the land.'

The Bulwark points to the achievement of *Catholic Action* in ensuring that bills and Acts have been passed in Parliament which have been beneficial to the Roman Catholic Church in spite of her minority status in the land. 'What is most notable in the examination of these items of legislation is that at times of great political and economic stress, when the minds of the people of this country were concentrated on other things, Rome stepped in and used these situations to her advantage.' (*The Bulwark*: 17 George IV Bridge, Edinburgh)

Education

The Education Act, of 1918, was brought in as the First World War ground to its exhausted halt. It created what is often referred to as a kind of religious apartheid by separating schools into denominations alongside the state system. Roman Catholicism aims everywhere, as 'the one true church,' to control all education, whether within its membership or not. Pope Pius XI in his encyclical, On the Education of Youth, declared in 1929; 'As for the scope of the Church's educative mission, it extends over all people without any limitations, according to Christ's command: 'Teach ye all nations.' Nor is there a power which can oppose it or prevent it.' Pope John XXIII said much the same thing on 30th December, 1959. As Professor Loraine Boettner stated in his scholarly book *Roman Catholicism*;

'The Roman Church does not hesitate to claim openly, even in the Protestant and democratic states, that education is exclusively a function of the Roman Catholic Church, as indeed it also claims that preaching and the administration of the sacraments are functions of the Roman Church only. This claim implies that education should be denied to all those outside the Roman Church, or only granted to the children of non-Romanist parents on the condition that they are placed under the instruction of Roman Catholic teachers. And indeed this is the policy that the Roman Church puts into effect in areas where she is in control – another means by which Rome seeks to maintain control over the people.'

'The ideal towards which the Roman Church strives is found in Spain where, under a Concordat with the Vatican, the schools are financed by the government while the Church supervises the curriculum, selects the teachers, and directs the administration of the schools. Protestant schools have always been prohibited. Why should anyone believe that the Roman Catholic Church, wherever it holds sway, would be satisfied with anything less?' (Loraine Boettner: *Roman Catholicism*, Banner of Truth Trust, 1962)

HM The Queen and Her Oath

Most British people have now lost sight of the fact that the Coronation Oath has for long been to defend and protect our Protestant Faith and 'to maintain to the utmost of the Sovereign's power the *Protestant Reformed religion* established by law.'

This is partly because Her Majesty the Queen has departed from her oath to the extent that she now does not defend what is widely accepted as the Christian religion, let alone the Protestant Reformed faith. The Daily Telegraph's religious correspondent, Damian Thompson, writing under the headline, 'Royal approval for Koran at abbey', noted that, in the unlikely setting of Westminster Abbey, the Queen and Prince of Wales listened intently as Muslim,

Hindu, Sikh and Buddhist leaders read or chanted from the sacred texts of their faiths, marking the beginning of 1991's Commonwealth Day Observance, which went ahead in its customary multi-faith format. According to some observers, the presence of the Prince as well as the Queen was a clear sign of Royal disapproval of the protests of evangelical Christians, in particular a petition organised by Anglican Tony Higton. In 1992, another petition, this time signed by 2000 evangelical clergymen received a similar response.

In the light of the Duke of Edinburgh's backing of the *International Sacred Literature Trust*, the Queen's strong approval of multi-faith services and Prince Charles' very public espousal of strands of New Age thought, parliament and the nation need to be reminded of the Coronation Oath.

Northern Ireland and the IRA

Many people in Northern Ireland have not lost sight of the sovereign's oath and the constitutional responsibility to uphold the Protestant Reformed Faith established by law.

Whilst excesses of Protestant reaction, cannot be condoned, these Ulster people are unable to understand why the Vatican does not act firmly against the IRA terrorists. Many of them argue that a word from the Pontiff to the priesthood, the threat of excommunication for the murderers of innocents, and the discontinuing of funerals for dead terrorists, would swiftly bring peace to Ireland. The absence of any such sanctions is significant to say the least. *Sunday Telegraph* Editor, Peregrine Worsthorne, expressed the same thought in his February 1991 leader, *The Ugly Face of Islam*: 'For years there has been no credible Islamic condemnation of terrorism. One could say the same thing about the Roman Catholic Church's attitude to terrorism in Ireland.'

The International Herald Tribune revealed that at Strasbourg, in 1988, Ian Paisley accused the Pope of having sent crucifixes to the IRA hunger strikers.(*The International Herald Tribune*: 12th October, 1988) This was reported in only one of the British newspapers at that time, and has not been denied to date. At the time of the hunger strikes, in

April 1981, the Vatican intervened in the political process much to the embarrassment of the British government. The intervention involved Cardinal Caseroli (Secretary of State at the Vatican), Cardinal Magee (the Pope's private secretary), Cardinals Hume and O'Faich (Primates of England and Ireland), the Papal Nuncios of the UK and Ireland, as well as representatives of the British Government. (*Pontiff*: G. Thomas & M. Morgan-Witts 1983)

Meanwhile those sympathetic to the plight of Ulster continue to wonder why the media so regularly features Roman Catholic prelates as spokesmen for the public outrage and for the condemnation of IRA violence; especially as there are so many instances of priests who seem to be supportive of the terrorists. For example the Sunday Express on 17th May, 1987 printed the eulogy given by Fr Brian McNeice at a Requiem Mass for IRA mass murderer Patrick Kelly: 'He was an upright and truthful man who loved his family, his Irish culture, his faith and his country'.

People also wonder how and why a priest apparently deeply involved in IRA terrorism could have been allowed to go entirely free. The conduct of the governments of Belgium & Ireland, two of Europe's most Roman Catholic countries, in relation to the Patrick Ryan extradition, following his hunger strike, again gives a glimpse of the shadow of Rome. Many people are puzzled and distressed that the sensational disclosure that the former priest used the Vatican bank to smuggle IRA funds, was so low key in the British press. The Sunday Times of 4th December, 1988 gave little space to report that British Intelligence had uncovered an IRA network, which included Ryan, and which had infiltrated and used Catholic Church banks world wide. Tens of millions of pounds are said to have been moved through terrorist accounts to finance IRA controlled businesses. Patrick Ryan has sued the British government for £1 million in libel damages, because judgments given in Ireland can be enforced in Britain under European legislation. The newspapers, according to the *Sunday Times* have made statements, no doubt drawing on information supplied by the government which they are now unable to defend. They may have to pay out millions, which no doubt would go straight into the pockets of the IRA. The reader may conclude that to be employed in Special Branch or other intelligence services must be very demoralising at times.

Those with memories long enough can recall a remarkably similar apparent suppression of news, following a major disclosure in *The Irish Press* of 26th May 1933. The story told (for the first time after 17 years) how, three weeks before the 'Easter week' uprising of 1916, Pope Benedict XV received a mission from the Irish Volunteer Executive headed by George Noble, Count Plunkett. Details of the insurrection were discussed with the Pope and the rebellion was blessed with 'his Apostolic Benediction on the men who were facing death for Ireland's liberty.'

The Irish Press disclosure revealed that the blessing of the Irish rebellion coincided with the receiving of the British envoy to the Vatican. Observers at that time felt that the whole press of the land should have been expected to clamour with indignation against such hypocrisy. But not a word! Strangely, as with Ryan in 1988, only *The Times* and perhaps two other papers reproduced the item a day late and without comment of any kind. The news was simply smothered.

Another example of apparent news suppression of which we have a clear record relates to when R.H.S. Crossman, then an Oxford Don and later a Minister in Harold Wilson's Government, broadcast from Berlin as a BBC correspondent in 1934. Describing unsettled conditions in Germany and Austria following Hitler's Great Blood Purge, he stated that wherever he went he was met with the indignant declaration that 'the Pope was behind all the trouble.' Immediately he mentioned the Pope there was dead silence on the wireless. Mr Crossman's talk was omitted from *The Listener*. Several people wrote to the BBC requesting copies of the complete talk but were refused any further information. (Albert Close: *Jesuit Plots from Elizabethan to Modern Times*, Protestant Truth Society)

If such news is being restricted under D notice regulations, then the very big question that emerges is who is doing the regulating and for whom?

The loss of public confidence in both police and judiciary,

following the release of the Guildford four and the Birmingham six, is a major victory for the IRA and is seen as serving the wider objective of weakening resistance to the yielding of our country's institutions to European federalism.

Chapter 10

Vatican Below the Surface

Dialogue, political and ecumenical is taking place continuously all over the world. There is that uneasy feeling that, in terms of real power exercised, we see but the tip of the iceberg. Glimpses of what might be lurking underneath come to the surface from time to time.

According to *The Economist*, in December 1988; 'the Catholic church was prominently involved in the struggle that toppled the dictatorship of President Ferdinand Marcos'. (*The Economist*: 24th December, 1988)

The Evening Standard, referring to the 1986 gathering of world Ecumenical leaders at Assisi, recorded that: '... guerrilla groups and militias in at least ten different countries agreed to honour the Pope's 24 hours of peace.' (*The Evening Standard*: 27th October, 1986) This extraordinary exercise of power over peace seems to anticipate the fulfillment of the Marian prophecy from Fatima which is the central vision for Pope John Paul's Pontificate. He believes that there will be a reappearance of the Virgin Mary, with great signs and wonders to convince the world of Papal spiritual leadership as a precursor to a period of peace. Many would agree that this is just what is predicted in the Scriptures.

Opus Dei

Another glimpse of power rarely visible relates to the relatively new right-wing organisation, *Opus Dei*, with which Roberto Calvi had dealings. 'Described by Italian politicians as a Holy Mafia, this secretive organisation operates as a kind of spiritual, 'militant tendency'. Pope John Paul II seems to have taken it under his wing, and in 1982 he made it a personal prelature. The organisation reports direct into the Vatican, to the Pope's prelate, Monsignor Alcaro del Portillo.' (*Daily Telegraph*, 8th May, 1986)

The prelature was an unprecedented step taken by the Polish Pope, giving him control personally of an organisation outside the whole Diocesan structure of the Church and independent of its Orders. It may be that Pope John Paul took the step in an attempt to counter-balance the formidable and growing power of the Jesuits.

Monsignor del Portillo was nominated 'Bishop for Life' by the Pope in December 1990 and made immune from the Canon Law rule requiring his resignation at the age of 75. Also in December 1990, the state of Italy published a decree of 'official recognition' of the organisation as a 'moral public entity.' The timing of the declaration was described on both sides of the Tiber as 'coincidental' and came five years after the Italian Parliament opened an enquiry into Opus.

An off-shoot of the Jesuits, founded in 1928, Opus Dei has been described as a quasi-diocese, covering the entire world and not defined by territory. It claims a membership of 75,000 in 80 countries and 1400 priests. (*The Universe*, 16th December, 1990) Articles have appeared in the press expressing the deep concern of parents whose sons have been recruited by Opus Dei and entirely lost to their families, apparently becoming entirely different personalities. The degree of secrecy that is involved comes across as sinister. An excerpt from a *Sydney Morning Herald* feature on this powerful and highly favoured organisation helps us to see why this is so: 'Numenaries are expected not only to take three monastic vows of chastity and obedience. ... This includes one session of self-flagellation a week with a variation with the cat-o'nine tails and the wearing of two hours a day of the cilis, a metal chain with links turned inward held in place by a thong. This is worn about the upper thigh so that it and the injuries it causes are not seen. The minimum recruiting age is 14½. The founder, Monsignor Escriva, said he received all this direct from God by a vision.' Escriva's cause for Sainthood has been advanced with unusual enthusiasm by the present Pope. The Spanish founder's controversial beatification in May 1992, the swiftest in modern times, has caused great concern and resentment within the Roman Catholic institution.

Committed Catholics in High Places

The rise of Roman Catholics in disproportionately high numbers to positions of ascendancy and great power, which in many spheres may be dominant, is seen by concerned Protestants as another hidden factor to be reckoned with. This is a very sensitive and invidious area, one which requires discernment and discretion and a constant guard against discrimination.

Over fifty per cent of recruits to the United States military academies are now Roman Catholic according to 1988 figures released by the Catholic Chaplain Recruitment Vicar for the military services. The number of Catholics in the United States House of Representatives increased from 82 in 1950 to 142 in 1986. Catholics occupy key positions in the Executive Branch, the Judiciary, the State Department, the delegation at the United Nations, in the CIA, FBI and the Department of Immigration.

Immigration policy in the USA is sharply increasing the Roman Catholic proportion of the population, a fact made politically visible by the fast rising importance of the Hispanic vote. This is to be seen within the wider context of continuing Papal prohibition of birth control throughout the Catholic world. The population of the continent of South America, for example, has doubled during the last generation. There are those who have made a study of Vatican global strategy who maintain that Vatican opposition to abortion and to birth control, as well as to homosexuality, has little to do with the sanctity of human life and Biblical ordinance. They believe that the real reason is that each new life adds to the 'Catholic army' and contributes to the funding of the Church. As discussed in an earlier chapter, the fact that birth control among Catholics in the major Protestant countries usually has only token opposition from the Church adds substance to this belief.

In Canada, it is now necessary to be bilingual to be employed in immigration, and other government departments, and thus a disproportionate number of recruits are Roman Catholics from Quebec and elsewhere. This bilingual policy brought in by Pierre Eliot Trudeau has led to most key positions in government and the bureaucracy being held by bilinguals and usually Quebecois Roman Catholics. This process has been encouraged and accelerated by Catholic Prime Minister, Brian Mulroney.

Quebec, threatened to secede if her demands were not met by the rest of the country in a new meddlesome Constitution. The man placed in charge of the Constitutional crisis was former Prime Minister and Foreign Secretary, Roman Catholic, Joe Clark. The people of Canada, at the October 1992 referendum decided that the Quebecois were asking too much.

Leadership of the old Dominion Commonwealth countries by serious Roman Catholics is not confined to Canada. New Zealand Premier, James Bolger, is devout in his faith, and presumably in his loyalty to the Supreme Pontiff. Australian Prime Minister, Paul Keating, is also Roman Catholic.

Espionage and Shielding of War Criminals

In the book, *The Vatican Papers*, published in 1982, Nino Lo Bello claims that 'the Vatican has the most efficient and widespread spy network in the whole world, outclassing even the Russian KGB.' He states that this group of espionage agents came to be known by the Popes as Sodalitium Pianum, and more widely as 'God's Underground,' and it may include any priest, nun and monk anywhere on earth. He argues that among this faithful army of more than 2.5 million people there are many full-time trained agents.

> 'What do agents do but infiltrate other organisations, and what organisations would Catholic spies infiltrate if not other churches, especially true churches of Jesus Christ.'

Catholic expert, Avro Manhattan, who died in November 1990, supports Lo Bello's definition; 'It's no exaggeration to say that the secretariat of the State of the Vatican has in every devout Catholic access to a potential source of news, and in every intelligent priest a trained informer. Whatever is judged useful from village or parish, is imparted to the local hierarchy, whence it is passed to the bishop, who, in turn, takes it to the Vatican. When to this is added the sundry information collected by the numerous semi-religious institutions operating in Christian and non Christian countries, through Catholic laymen who are organised into societies or into political parties in close touch with and often under the direction of priests, as well as the information gathered through the usual diplomatic channels, it then becomes evident that the Secretariat of State of the Vatican is one of the best informed news agencies in the world, if not the best.' (*The Dollar and the Vatican*: A. Manhattan 1988)

Other Vatican observers draw attention to the moles buried deep within the espionage networks of the CIA, KGB, MI5 and other secret services throughout the world, whose ultimate allegiance may well be determined by a secret oath of loyalty to the papal system. It seems likely that Mossad, the Israeli intelligence service, widely regarded as dollar for dollar far and away the most effective, is the least penetrated in this way.

Papal links with the CIA have been strong since the Agency superseded the OSS after World War Two. For example the Knights of Malta, otherwise known as the Sovereign Military Order of Malta (SMOM), which acts and is recognised as a government in itself, has clear bonds with the CIA. In 1948, the Order, which is totally loyal to the Pope, issued one of its most prestigious awards of honour, the Gran Croci al Merito Con Placa, to General Richard Gehlen, head of Adolph Hitler's anti-Soviet Spy network. After the war Gehlen was hired by the CIA along with other Nazi war criminals. The former head of the Knights of Malta in the USA, J. Peter Grace, the industrialist, was personally involved in getting Nazis out of Europe and into America and helping to reduce their prison sentences, as well as employing them in the giant family organisation.

Two CIA Directors have been Knights of Malta, namely John and William Casey; and George Rocca, Deputy Chief of Counter-Intelligence also held membership. According to writer, Kathleen Hayes; 'more than adequate information exists to link the SMOM, the ultra-right wing, the Vatican and the CIA to the Iran-Contra Affair. Behind what was made to appear as an anti-Communist effort in Central America, was another plot. Evidence from the hearings clearly indicated that a shadowy government within the U.S. government was in operation. Exactly what it was attempting to accomplish remains murky.' (*Knights of Malta Comprise a Shadowy Society. NFI Trumpet*, Kathleen R. Hayes 1987) Oliver North's attorney for the Iran-Contra hearings, Brendon Sullivan, is a Knight of Malta, as is his firm's prestigious proprietor, Bennett Williams. The involvement of the Vatican and the Jesuits in Nicaraguan politics is referred to elsewhere in this book.

The Times reported in 1987 that former Gestapo chief Klaus Barbie's[1] 'principal collaborator' in German-occupied France, Paul Touvier, was 'shielded by the Church and the Catholic hierarchy of Lyons,' and in his deal with the Vatican, had handed over 'all the militia money from the looting of Jewish homes and properties.' (*The Times*, 18th May, 1987). *The Daily Mail* recalled that Touvier was twice sentenced to death for war crimes. First in 1945, when he disappeared under church protection, and then in 1947. Under the French statute of limitations, these sentences expired in 1967 and five years later, after intensive church lobbying, President Pompidou pardoned him. The *Daily Mail* columnist, Geoffrey Levy, went on to point out that the people of Lyon believe, 'quite simply, that Touvier had been sheltered and helped all these years because of what he knows about the church.' (*Daily Mail*, 14th July, 1989)

The Vatican Papers joins with other accounts of the Nazi

---

[1] It is instructive to note that before his arrest, Barbie, who had been recruited by the CIA after the war, was heavily involved in arms deals as well as in Bolivian politics with Lucio Gelli, Grand Master, and other members of Masonic Lodge P2. (David Yallop: *In God's Name*.)

'monastery escape route', managed by a Croatian priest and used by many of the Nazis including Martin Bormann, attired as a Jesuit priest, and Adolph Eichmann who escaped to Argentina with a Vatican passport. This book also examines the close connections between the Vatican and ODESSA, the secret organisation of former Nazis.

The Independent of 6th January, 1988, records Cardinal Franz Konig, former Archbishop of Vienna, quoted in the Israeli newspaper *Yediot Ahronath* as saying:

After the war, senior churchmen helped Nazi criminals flee. 'I personally know two ... an Austrian and a German ... both hold to this day high posts in the Vatican.'

Cardinal Konig also stated that the Catholic Church in Austria bore part of the responsibility for Nazi crimes against the Jews. The Holocaust museum exhibition in Jerusalem begins with a picture and description of the Roman Catholic Bishops of Austria at the *Anschluss*, welcoming Hitler's legions as liberators and bestowing their Apostolic blessing on the Nazis.

The 'monastery escape route' is also known as 'the rat route'. An article in *The Jerusalem Post* of December 15th 1990, by Alexander Zvielli, described how United States secret agent Vincent La Vista discovered, in the Spring of 1947, that the Vatican and the International Red Cross were the main forces behind the illegal emigration of Nazis from Germany to Latin America via Italy. La Vista reported: 'further investigation has established that in those Latin American countries where the Church is a controlling or dominating factor, the Vatican has brought pressure to bear which has resulted in the foreign missions of those countries taking an attitude almost favouring the entry into their country of former Nazis and former Fascists or other political groups so long as they are anti-Communist. ... The Vatican was of course the largest single organisation involved in this illegal emigration. It provided transport, hide-out and financial support. On the other hand, such groups, the Vatican included, did not operate without help; they had necessarily, at various times and under certain conditions, to make use of the International Red Cross.'

Chapter 11

Papal Power

Roman Catholicism is seen as a dual system. It is both a Church and a global, political power. Within or without the reciprocal 'Mutual Assured Destruction' capability of the superpowers, the Vatican wields the greatest political power on the face of the earth.

> 'Although without armies, navies and super hydrogen bombs, the Vatican has more power at its disposal than if it had the greatest military capability. The Pope's government is as important as that of the USA, of Russia or of China except that territorially and spiritually it is far larger and it exerts more influence than the three combined.' (A. Manhattan: *Vatican Imperialism* in the 20th Century: 1965 Zondervan)

Like other great multinational organizations, the Roman Catholic Church has a planned long-term strategy. The papacy has continuity of a kind that no other organization or nation on earth can match. Nations and giant corporations are subjected to economic imponderables or electoral changes, but the Vatican is not constrained in this way. She is able to plan well ahead. Corporations plan five or ten years ahead, the Vatican is able to construct a strategy over many decades and can exercise the clout to implement it.

History shows how Rome throughout the centuries has been able to steadily accumulate power and influence, unless or until she over-reaches herself or decides there is a need to change direction.

For example, under Pius IX in the late 19th century she over-reached herself and lost the papal states and much of her temporal power. In this century, in the '60s, under John XXIII and Paul VI, believing she was no longer backing a winner, she totally changed direction. Pius XII's policy of opposing Communism, first by backing the Fascist dictators and afterwards through 'the Cold War' (spawning the rabid anti-Communism of such as committed Roman Catholic senator Joe McCarthy), was abandoned. The Vatican had concluded that it was backing the wrong side. In came a brand new two-pronged strategy, both political and ecclesiastical, temporal and spiritual. Co-existence with both communism and capitalism, coupled with acceptance of Protestantism and other heretical religions (or 'separated brethren'), would provide the new route towards world dominion.

As Krushchev was turning away from Stalinism, so in the late 1950s were Vatican strategists turning away from Pius XII's policies. As the final plans for Vatican II were laid, so was the rapprochement taking place, which would lead to the forming of the 'Vatican-Moscow alliance'. After the failed attempts of more than three decades of political interference to oppose Marxism, the Vatican set about working with it. As we have now seen, Marxism did not fare well with this new arrangement.

The new face of the papacy, conciliatory and more human, exemplified by John XXIII, was to be the face shown to the world, that of Vatican II and the new ecumenism, and soon also that of liberation theology and the new politics. Behind the face is the strategy and a plan to 'evangelize the world.' This also includes the conversion to the Mother Church of Soviet Russia, as promised by Our Lady of Fatima. We shall be looking further at the Vatican strategy in the chapter 'Peace and *Evangelization 2000*.'

Economic Power

The Roman Church's unparalleled wealth is legendary, although in these days of careful image building, the Vatican is at pains to deny it, and even to plead poverty. The frequent appearance of articles in the newspapers about the hard-pressed position of Vatican finances help to foster this impression. Few people outside the system realise the prodigious capacity of the Church to raise funds. In his 1957 book *The Vatican contre la France*, Edmond Paris described; 'The gigantic financial power which the Vatican represents in the world today. Is it realised for instance that one third of the land in Spain is hers? – and that in South America she owns vast expanses? And this does not include innumerable other properties spread over the rest of the globe. ... Already Peter's pence from 400 million faithful, legacies, offerings and Masses (all geared to helping loved ones through the pains of purgatory), ensure the Holy See a revenue that may be termed astronomical ... One cannot help noting that, from the temporal point of view, the Church's most beneficial years were those of the Second World War – at the end of which we have seen, facing a Europe that was bloodstained, ruined and completely plundered by the Nazis, the Vatican overflowing with the most fabulous riches.'

'The love of money is the root of all evil.' (1 Timothy 6:10); and the love of money is the corrupted root of Christianity of the Roman kind. Candles, holy water, relics, indulgences, Masses for the living and the dead, intercessory prayers by Mary and the Saints, all are enormous sources of revenue for the Vatican. The income generated for the Church of Rome by the fear of 'the pains of purgatory', by itself, is simply awesome.

Purgatory, first adopted in the 6th century pontificate of Gregory the Great, and defined in the modern *Catholic Catechism* as that state of temporary suffering for those who die guilty of 'venial sins', or who haven't fully satisfied for the punishment due to their 'forgiven sins', flies in the face of all the Scriptures. Christians have complete assurance from the Bible that those who have put their faith in Christ and have accepted Him as Saviour and Lord, have been entirely and forever purged and cleansed of all sin and guilt, by Him and only Him. *The blood of Jesus, His son, cleanseth us from all sin* (1 John 1:7) ... *and when he had by himself purged our* sins... (Hebrews 1:3) ... *and this man, after he had offered one sacrifice for sins for ever, sat down on the right hand of God.* (Hebrews 10:12). Jesus' saying, *it is finished.* (John 19:30), before he died, meant that he had accomplished all; no sin remained which was not purged.

Thus, purgatory, as a concept is entirely unbiblical, but it has been extraordinarily profitable. It became official dogma of the Chuch of Rome at the *Council of Florence* in 1439, and since then has extended the Mother Church's power over the souls of men and over their giving. No single idea in the whole of history has ever raised so much money.

Another attempt at appraisal of the wealth of the Roman Church was made in 1983 by American author, Avro Manhattan:

> 'The Vatican's treasure of solid gold has been estimated by the United Nation's World Magazine to amount to several billion dollars. A large bulk of this is stored with the United States Federal Reserve Bank, while banks in England and Switzerland hold the rest. But this is just a small portion of the wealth of the Vatican, which in the US alone, is greater than that of the five wealthiest giant corporations of this country. When to that is added all the real estate, property, stocks and shares abroad, then the staggering accumulation of the wealth of the Catholic Church becomes so formidable as to defy any rational assessment.' (*Vatican Billions: Avro Manhattan*)

Such wealth and a matchless organisational structure has enabled the Vatican's influence and will to be exercised invisibly and variously by Orders, such as the Jesuits and Opus Dei, the Knights of Columbus and the Knights of Malta, the Knights of St John of Jerusalem, the Knights Templar, the Legionaires of Christ and the Prieure de Sion (a Templar Order involved with hermetic Freemasonry and with close ties to the House of Hapsberg) and the Blue Army. Such organisations, legions of the Papacy, zealously work for the Roman Catholic institution, and within them, allegiance to the Pope takes precedence over every other loyalty. In common one with another and with Freemasonry too, they possess a very acceptable public image, a secret oath, and higher echelons which are kept secret often even from their own lower levels. At the highest levels there is participation in other secret organisations such as the Rosicrucians and the Illuminati.

We have looked briefly at Opus Dei in a previous chapter and the chapter which follows is about the Jesuits. The Blue Army is a worldwide crusade of some twenty million zealous Catholics who are obedient to the requirements of Our Lady of Fatima, wearing the Brown Scapular and repeating the Rosary frequently. The Knights of Columbus have a membership of 1.2 million, 5400 subordinate councils and according to the Roman Catholic Directory, 'a comprehensive programme against subversive activities.' The secret oath for the 4th Degree of the Knights of Columbus, unless it has been changed, includes the following; 'Therefore, to the utmost of my power, I shall and will defend this doctrine (of the Pope's Vice-regency of Christ) and his Holiness' right and customs against all usurpers of the heretical or Protestant authority, whatever, especially the Lutheran Church of Germany, Holland, Denmark, Sweden and Norway, and the now pretended authority of the Church of England and Scotland, the branches of the same now established in Ireland, and on the continent of America and elsewhere. ... I do now renounce and disown any allegiance as due to any heretical king, prince or state named Protestant or Liberals or obedience to any of their laws, magistrates or officers. I do further declare, that I will help and assist and advise all or any of his Holiness' agents in any place wherever I shall be, and do my utmost to extirpate the heretical Protestant or Liberal doctrines and to destroy all their pretended powers, legal or otherwise.' (documented in the *United States Congressional record* 1913).

The Sinn Fein Oath is in many respects remarkably similar, although phrased in stronger language.

Chapter 12

The Jesuits Today

A vigilant Christian organisation CRIB, Catholic Research Information Bureau, sounded a strong and sober warning note; 'Don't be deceived. The Roman Church is like a chameleon. Tolerant, friendly, highly moral and authoritative in Protestant England and America; but where there is a Roman Catholic majority, she is very different and no friend of freedom, always blending in with the landscape, but never quite what she seems to be.'

H.G. Wells observed in his book, *Crux Ansata* that, 'Roman Catholicism presents many faces to the world, but everywhere it is systematic in its fight against freedom.'

The Jesuits, who originally implemented the Counter-Reformation by decree of the Council of Trent, are seen as continuing to do so in the present century with increasing success. Once counsellors to kings such as James II and Louis XIV, who held 'divine rights', the Jesuits very often master-minded the dramatic events of history by scheming and prompting backstage. Now they are making their come-back in positions of influence among our institutions. Many of them have been able to come out in the open, since in the current climate of spiritual indifference, they have little to hide. However, placed in key positions in religious broad-casting, in educational establishments (including Britain's top schools), even in evangelistic undertakings, they have been re-instated in a way that just decades ago would have seemed unthinkable.

At the head of the Society of Jesus is the Superior-

General, the supreme ruler over the Jesuits, often called 'The Black Pope.' The full extent of his power and influence over the Papacy can be known to very few, but it is more than possible that often it exceeds that of the Pope himself.

Notorious in the past, expelled from every country in Europe and banned from residence in England until 1902, the Jesuits have often been described as the 'secret army of the Papacy.' The preface to Edmund Paris' book *The Secret History of the Jesuits* includes a warning to the church which has been sounded many times in relation to the threat posed by the Counter-Reformation; 'The order of the Society of Jesus was founded by Ignatius Loyola to secretly accomplish two major goals for the Roman Catholic Institution. The first was to obtain universal political power; the second, to establish the universal church. The Reformation had seriously damaged the Roman system. The way forward, apart from the Inquisition, was by infiltration and penetration into every section of life, with the aim of enforcing the canons and doctrines and temporal power of the Pope. To that end Jesuits went to work, secretly infiltrating all Protestant groups, including families, places of work, hospitals, schools, colleges etc. Today the Jesuits have almost completed that mission. The Bible puts local church government into the hands of a godly pastor but the effect of Jesuit activity over the years has been to remove that power to the denominational Headquarters, to temporalise the church and thus to push Protestant denominations into the arms of the Vatican.' (*The Secret History of the Jesuits*: Edmund Paris, Chick Publications, Chino, California)

> '*For there are certain men crept in unawares, who were before of old ordained to this condemnation . . .*'
>
> Jude 4

Rev. J.A. Wylie, in *The History of Protestantism*, described the Jesuits thus:

'There was no tongue they could not speak, and no creed they could not profess, and thus there was no people among whom they might not sojourn and no church whose membership they might not enter and whose functions they might not discharge. They could execrate the Pope with the Lutheran, and swear the Solemn League with the Covenanter.' 'The Order of Jesus is never more formidable than when it appears to be least so. It is when Jesuits are stripped of all external means of doing harm that they devise the vastest schemes, and execute them with the most daring courage.' (Revd J.A. Wylie: *The History of Protestantism*)

In the *History of the Jesuits*, published in 1897, A. Nicolini revealed the four open classes of Jesuits and the fifth secret class who;

'by the confession of Fr Pellini, constitute the strength and power of the society. Nor does the agent of Rome, and above all, the Jesuit, expound at once the whole system of his religion, such as it is; but, with diabolical dexterity he first insinuates himself into the confidence of the man he has marked as a proselyte, captivates his benevolence by all sorts of arts, and then, step by step, he leads him as a convert into the fold of the modern Babylon.'

In 1551, Secret Instructions, sent from the Council of Trent to the Jesuits in Paris, were intercepted on the person of Thomas Heath, who was a Jesuit professing the highest style of Puritanism. These instructions set forth the most effective way of undermining and destroying the Church of England;

'Ye are not to preach all after one method, but observe the place wherein you come. If Lutherism be prevalent, then preach Calvinism; if Calvinism, then Lutheranism; if in England then either of them, or John Huss's opinions, Anabaptism, or any that are contrary to the Holy See or of St Peter, by which your function will not be suspected, and yet you may still act on the interest of Mother-Church; there being as the Council are agreed on, no better way to demolish that Church (the Church of England) of heresy, but by mixture of doctrines, and by adding of ceremonies more than at present permitted.' (Albert Close: *Rome's Fight for the British Throne*, Wycliffe Press, London)

According to the French writer Adolphe Michel, Voltaire estimated the number of books written about the Jesuits over the years to be around 6000 at the end of the 18th century. In the 19th century books and sermons countering the Jesuits and their activities were published in profusion. Nowadays they are few and far between. It seems that innumerable such works have gone out of print and disappeared from the bookshelves. In theological colleges and public libraries, it is now hard to find any history of the Jesuits beyond the beginning of the 17th century. Most books on the counter-reformation are written by Roman Catholics, many by the Jesuits themselves. Given that the Society of Jesus, today possibly more than ever, is the leading wing of the Roman Church, all of this needs explanation and attention. Protestant watchmen believe that the Jesuits have accomplished a remarkable feat in a relatively short time span in ridding schools, universities and theological colleges of almost all historical literature written from a Protestant viewpoint.

Indoctrination and Obedience

Education is the key to Jesuitism itself. Nicolini again:

'The most striking characteristic of Jesuit education, as we have already frequently remarked; was, and still is, that almost all the persons educated in their colleges consider themselves in a certain way attached to the order, and to the end of their lives work to their utmost for its aggrandisement. And this art of binding to their Society all their disciples, makes the Jesuits powerful and dangerous, especially in those countries where they are adverse to the government or to a class of citizens. **We insist on this consideration**.'

130

Examples of this binding or indoctrination are readily to be found in the *Spiritual Exercises* of founder Ignatius Loyola. *In Rules for thinking with the Church*, the instruction is: 'always to be ready to obey with mind and heart, setting aside all judgment of one's own, the true Spouse of Christ, our Holy Mother, our infallible and orthodox mistress, the Catholic Church, whose authority is exercised over us by the hierarchy.'

Another principle laid down by Loyola may cause the reader to gasp:

> 'That we may be altogether of the same mind and in conformity with the Church herself, if she shall have defined anything to be black, which to our eyes appears to be white, we ought in like manner to pronounce it to be black.'

The total 'obedience' required from those who accept the Constitution and swear the Jesuit Oath is such that 'they must allow themselves to be borne and ruled by divine providence working through their superiors, exactly as if they were a corpse which suffers itself to be borne and handled in any way whatsoever; or just an old man's stick which serves him who holds it in his hand wherever and whatever purpose he wish to use it.' (*Documents of the Christian Church*: Sir Henry Bettenson pp 361–63)

Such training and discipline and total submission to the Order, allied to ruthless single-mindedness, have brought worldly dividends in the exercise of absolute power in this century, as well as in the last.

Abraham Lincoln and The Jesuits

Former Roman Catholic priest, Charles Chiniquy, who during the 1860s led almost all the Catholic population of St Anne, Illinois to trusting Christ alone; was a friend and confidante of President Abraham Lincoln. In his book *50 Years in the Church of Rome*, he describes his last meeting with Lincoln before the assassination. The President spoke of his presentiment that God 'will call me to Him through the hand of an assassin,' and expressed his feelings and revealed a very deep faith:

'I see the storm coming, and I know that His hand is in it ... I believe I am ready! I am nothing, but truth is everything! I know that I am right , because I know that liberty is right: for Christ teaches it, and Christ is God.'

He spoke of his impending death, following news he had just received of the letter of Pope Pius IX to Jefferson Davis, in support of the South's cause in the Civil War. He knew that the publication of this letter was his death warrant.

'So many plots have been made against my life, that it is a real miracle that they have all failed, when we consider that the great majority of them were in the hands of the skilful Roman Catholic murderers, evidently trained by Jesuits. ... The Jesuits are so expert in those deeds of blood, that Henry IV said that it is impossible to escape them, and he became their victim, though he did all that could be done to protect himself. My escape from their hands, since the letter of the pope to Jeff Davis has sharpened a million of daggers to pierce my breast, would be more than a miracle. But just as the Lord heard no murmur from the lips of Moses when He told him that he had to die, before crossing the Jordan, for the sins of his people; so I hope and pray that He will hear no murmur from me when I fall for my nation's sake.'

President Lincoln was assassinated in Washington on the 14th of April 1865. Brigadier General Thomas Harris, a member of the Military Commission that tried and condemned the conspirators found guilty of the crime, was convinced of the complicity of the Roman Catholic hierarchy in the assassination, and its responsibiity for it. He wrote that there was 'positive evidence that the Jesuit fathers engaged in preparing young men for the priesthood away out in the village of St Joseph, in far off Minnesota, were in correspondence with their brethren in Washington City, and had been informed that the plan to assassinate the President had been matured, the agents for its accomplishment had been found, the time for its execution had been set, and so sure were they of its accomplishment, that they could announce it as already done, three or four hours before it had been consummated.' (Brigadier General Thomas Harris: *Rome's Responsibility for the Assassination of Abraham Lincoln*, Pilgrim Brethren Press, Petersberg, Ohio)

The Nazis and the Catholic Hierarchy

Hitler and Himmler were greatly influenced by the Jesuits, as was Mussolini, whose Father Confessor was a Jesuit. Dr J.H. Lehmann, points out in his book *Behind the Dictators* that the Jesuit Father Staempfle wrote *Mein Kampf* for Hitler. The 'ghost-writing' of Staempfle argues in *Mein Kampf* in favour of the indisputability of Catholic dogmas and of the intolerant attitude of Catholic education, as well as the necessity of blind faith and of the personal infallibility of the Pope. (J.H. Lehmann: *Behind the Dictators*, Agrora Publishing Company, New York, 1942).

Edmond Paris relates in *The Vatican Against Europe* that Hitler's associate Hermann Rauschning recalls Hitler as saying that he learned most of all from the Jesuit order; 'So far there has been nothing more imposing on earth than the hierarchical organisation of the Roman Catholic Church. A good part of that organisation I have transported to my own party. ... I will tell you a secret. I am founding an order.' (*Hitler m'a dit*: H. Rauschning, *Editions Co-operation*, 1939)[1]

Hitler was also quoted as saying of Heinrich Himmler; 'In Himmler I see our Ignatius de Loyola.' (*Libres Propos*, Flammarion, Paris 1952). Walter Schellenberg (like Joseph Goebbels, Jesuit-educated), who led the SD or Sicherheitsdienst, the Security Service of the SS, and was sentenced to death at Nuremberg for crimes against humanity, stated that 'The SS Organisation has been constituted by Himmler according to the principles of the Jesuit Order. Their regulations and the Spiritual Exercises prescribed by Ignatius of Loyola were the model Himmler tried to copy exactly.' (*The Vatican Against Europe*: Edmond Paris, Wycliffe Press, London, 1961)

[1] 'For two years he (Hitler) attended classes at the Benedictine monastery at Lambach ... There he sang in the choir ...' (p.24 *The Rise and Fall of the Third Reich*, William L. Shirer: Pan Books)

Himmler, whose uncle, 'the Jesuit Father Himmler was the very eye and arm of Halke von Ledochowski, General of his order', according to author Edmond Paris, 'belonged to a family that was entirely devoted to the Church. His position as supreme chief of the SS was to be the equivalent of the "Jesuit's General", and the whole structure was a close imitation of the Catholic Church's hierarchical order.' (*The Vatican Against Europe*: Edmond Paris, Wycliffe Press, London, 1961)

The Nazi Party was brought to power through the acquiescence of the Catholic Central Party in Germany and the higher strategy of the Vatican. Instrumental in this strategy were Reich Chancellor Franz Von Papen and Papal Nuncio, Monsignor Pacelli, the future Pope Pius XII. Von Papen, owner of the Central party's official paper *Germania*, played a leading part in obtaining Hitler his two thirds majority, signed the law which made Hitler Head of State and also was responsible for the enormously important Concordat with the Pope in Rome in 1933. The Concordat was his most remarkable achievement and the culmination of his close working with Pacelli and the Vatican. Von Papen declared; 'The Third Reich is the first power in the world, not only to recognize, but to put into practice, the lofty principles of the Papacy.'

Pacelli, as Pius XII, became notorious for his silence with regard to Nazi atrocities and Von Papen, for his success in avoiding responsibility for them. Pius XII is high up on the present Pope's short-list for canonisation and Von Papen, who incredibly was acquitted at Nuremberg, was later appointed Papal Chamberlain to Pope John XXIII.

The Exercise of Power – The Apparatus of 'Catholic Action'

In his book *Memorial of the Captivity of Napoleon at St Helena* (Vol 2), French General Montholon gave his description of the Society of Jesus; 'The Jesuits are a military organisation, not a religious order. Their chief is general of an army, not the mere father abbot of a monastery. And the aim of this organisation is **power**. Power in its most despotic exercise. Absolute power, universal power, power to control the world by the volition of a single man. Jesuitism is the most absolute of despotisms; and at the same time the greatest and most enormous of abuses.'

Many Protestant 'watchmen' see the Jesuits as just as powerful and active as ever today. Writing in 1965 Avro Manhattan, an authority on Roman Catholicism in politics, described them as 'the ecclesiastical storm-troopers of the Catholic Church,' and remarked that 'it is most significant that in two traditionally English speaking Protestant countries, Great Britain and the USA, they have their largest contingents.' (*Vatican Imperialism in the Twentieth Century*: Zondervan, Grand Rapids, Michigan.)

Jesuits occupy posts at the highest levels of influence in government, although they are not easily identified. One example, Vernon Walters was a roving ambassador for successive United States Administrations and top-level negotiator for the White House for many years. In Washington he has steered a careful path avoiding calls to power and concentrating on serving men at the very top. He was educated at Stonyhurst College and at French Jesuit schools and was described by former Secretary of State, Alexander Haig, as 'like a member of the clergy in terms of his lifestyle.' Vernon Walters' most recent assignment has been as Ambassador to Germany leading up to re-unification and beyond.

Influence in the Church

Another former pupil of top Jesuit school, Stonyhurst College, is leading English Charismatic Charles Whitehead. In his testimony that he gives on the FGBMFI circuit, he has revealed and affirmed his Jesuit background. He is married to an Anglican and heads the Catholic Charismatic Renewal organisation in Britain and also for Northern Europe, for which he regularly reports to the Vatican. His para-Church activities, especially his role as President of an FGBMFI chapter have greatly influenced many Protestant leaders, who have been led in an ecumenical direction by him. Appearances on television in 1991 point the way to his arrival on the national stage as Catholic lay leader in the Charismatic Church as it emerges as a serious force under George Carey's ecumenical leadership.

David Alton, whose battle against abortion in Parliament has won him great influence among evangelicals, was baptised by Franciscan monks and educated by the Sisters of Mercy and the Jesuits. According to *Sunday Times* writer Elizabeth Grice, Alton mocks the suggestion that he is a member of the Roman Catholic mafia, taking his orders from Rome. He describes himself as an Ecumenical Christian and like Charles Whitehead is married to an Anglican; and although he worships mainly at Liverpool's Roman Catholic Cathedral, he also attends a Church of England church in Edge Hill.

'Many of the people who attended the rally which launched the new *Movement of Christian Democracy* in London, in November 1990, were pro-lifers who had made contact with David Alton's office during the Abortion Amendment campaign,' according to the Catholic newspaper, *The Universe*. Founded by Mr Alton and his Roman Catholic fellow MP, Ken Hargreaves, the Movement aims to 'bring Christian values back into British political life,' as well as 'to forge a valuable link with other Christian parties on the European mainland, such as those in Italy, Germany, Belgium, Luxemberg, Holland and Austria, together with their new counterparts in Hungary, Poland and Czechoslovakia.' (*Catholic Herald*: 10th August, 1990)

There is little doubt but that the solid post-War success of the Christian Democratic parties in Europe has convinced the Vatican that Social Democracy with a Christian label is the way forward, especially after the spectacular failure of Communism. The Jesuits, using 'Catholic Action' and other forms of political activity and pressure, have played the key role in bringing about these successes in Western Europe and are poised to do the same in the East. The Pope has specifically called on the Society of Jesus to train priests for Eastern Europe to give the Roman Catholic Church what *The European* described as 'a leading role in the political reform of Eastern Europe.' (*The European*: 14th-16th December 1990).

Time Magazine reported, in the same month that 'Jesuit experts met in Rome in mid-December 1990 to plan this job. The Jesuits, currently training 1.8 million students in colleges and schools throughout the world, are regarded as 'the intellectual elite who educate the cream of Catholic society, as well as being the largest missionary body in the Catholic Church.' (*Time Magazine*: 10th December, 1990)

Another Strategy, Another Ideology: Different Means, Same Ends

Whereas Christian Democracy has brought many dividends to the Vatican in Europe, the strategy for Central America implemented by the Jesuits has been more reliant on Marxism and 'Liberation Theology'. The Denver, Colorado-based organisation *Concerned Christians* drew attention to Jesuit activities in Latin American countries in 1989; 'Jesuits occupy high positions in the Sandanista government in Nicaragua, despite its Marxist leanings', reported the magazine *US News and World Report*. Others, having set up a network of 'worker priests', 'are deeply involved in revolutionary movements in El Salvador, Guatemala, Brazil and elsewhere.'

They play a key role in the major theological offensive which is bringing Marxism and Roman Catholicism together under the banner of 'Liberation Theology.' The Pope described Liberation Theology as 'not only orthodox but necessary, when purified of elements which can adulterate it'. It is widely seen by watchful Christians as what Jesuit-educated Marxist Fidel Castro[2] had called for at the end of the 1970's; 'a strategic alliance between religion and socialism, between religion and revolution.'

The 'Church' Militant

Cardinal Manning, leader of Catholicism in England at the end of the 19th century and a staunch supporter of Papal

---

[2] Castro's durability may be seen now as owing more to the Vatican than the Kremlin, to religion more than revolution or socialism.

Infallibility in 1870, spoke to the Jesuit 'fathers' in stirring fashion, calling them to battle and unmistakably laying out the strategy and plan of attack for the 20th century;

> 'Great is the prize for which you strive. Surely a soldier's eye and a soldier's heart would choose by intuition this field of England. None ampler or nobler could be found. It is an head of Protestantism, the centre of its movements and the stronghold of its power. Weakened in England, it is paralysed elsewhere. Conquered in England, it is conquered throughout all the world. Once overthrown here, all else is but a war of detail. All the roads of the world meet in one point, and this point reached, all the world is open to the Church's will.' (*Life of Cardinal Manning* by Edward Sheridan Purcell)

The Bible gives a clear warning;

> *For I know this, that after my departing shall grievous wolves enter in among you, not sparing the flock.*
>
> Acts 20:29

CRIB has also warned the church to be vigilant;

> 'Jesuits, or at least those with Jesuit training, for the first time in our history, are in the most influential leadership roles; as religious broadcasters, as chaplains in Britain's top schools and educational establishments and as speakers, teachers and organisers among the leading "para-church" organisations.
>
> Their sincerity and the courage of their convictions in relation to their cause is not to be questioned. This is the very thing that makes the situation so dangerous and why it is vital that "the watchman sound the alarm".
>
> The aim of the Papacy and its secret army is as it always has been, to gain world domination and every human subject to it. The Ecumenical movement was not founded on the free evangelical message of Christ and the outpouring of the Holy Spirit, but was spawned in the dark corridors of the Vatican by the Jesuit

General Bea. This movement is the latest expression of that system, spoken of in Scripture, which will be destroyed according to the fulfilment of God's will.' (Revelation 17:16, 17, 18)

The Scriptures carefully and repeatedly warn us of the deception in our midst;

> *'false brethren unawares brought in, who came in privily to spy out our liberty, which we have in Christ Jesus, that they might bring us into bondage.'*   Galatians 2:4

> *'For such are false apostles, deceitful workers, transforming themselves into the apostles of Christ. And no marvel; for Satan himself is transformed into an angel of light. Therefore it is no great thing if his ministers also be transformed as the ministers of righteousness; whose end shall be according to their works.'*
>   2 Corinthians 11:13–15

Chapter 13

'Martyrs' and 'Saints'?

We are living in a climate of increasing indifference towards our history. People believe 'today is what matters, yesterday is not relevant'. The spirit of the age has tuned us in to what is now and what is new. Materialism and a comfortable life seduce us into the conviction that we have progressed and evolved as human beings. This illusion is being fed by TV, today's household god, which is convincing us that we are in control of our planet and our destiny. Our advance as a civilization is not only in expertise and technology, but also in our approach to religion too. The church has caught hold of this new dynamic, perhaps from the world; the Lord is 'doing a new thing.' Renewal has rescued the Christians from the past, from all the unpleasantness, the strife and the blood-letting. The old conflicts over doctrine are no longer relevant. Those things which caused such division almost throughout the whole Christian era have no place on the agenda today. There is no need to think about them, or to talk about them or to teach our children about them in school. It is divisive and unloving to do so.

Resistance to Britain's Protestant Christian heritage, aspects of which are increasingly represented as offensive, is gathering strength. The 1988 year of anniversaries, during which Christians commemorated no fewer than ten important centenaries and jubilees relating to the history of the English Bible, was given very little coverage on TV or in the national press, although Her Majesty The Queen began

140

her 1988 Christmas message by stressing the importance to the nation of both 1588 and 1688, and spoke of how different our history would have been without the great events commemorated by the anniversaries.

One vital aspect of that heritage has been subtly undermined. Many of us were brought up to believe that the martyrs of our faith were those who died in the fire unable and unwilling to compromise their trust in the Scriptures, as the revealed Word of God. But in November 1987, in uncharacteristic fashion, the serious newspapers, TV and radio were giving prominent coverage to 'the honouring of English martyrs.'

Many whose attention had been captured by such headlines, and whose imagination had been fired in the classroom by accounts of the heroism of Cranmer, Latimer and Ridley, must have been startled to discover that they referred to 85 Roman Catholic 'heroes of resistance to the Protestant Reformation.' These men were beatified by the Pope in Rome in the presence of Anglican Bishop of Birmingham, Mark Santer. In a special message, Catholic Archbishop of Westminster, Cardinal Hume said carefully; 'the story of the martyrs must not be seen as an embarrassing episode, but must take its rightful place as an important part of our heritage.'

It is likely that policy-makers in Rome would be aware that only one Anglican Bishop since the war has attended a memorial service for any of the martyrs of the reformed faith.[1] The caution that characterised previous beatifications and canonisations in Protestant countries is no longer necessary. The number of canonisation processes has escalated dramatically during the last few years, including those carried out, for the first time in history, on foreign soil. In the single year 1982, for example, more causes were introduced than during the whole of the 1950s. (Peter Hebblethwaite: *In the Vatican* 1987). Pope John Paul II, in 12 years

---

[1] The lone exception was Dr Chavasse, Bishop of Rochester, who attended the 400th Anniversary Commemoration of the martyrdom of Latimer and Ridley at Oxford in 1955.

of his Papacy 'raised to the altars' more Saints of the Church than all his predecessors of this century combined. He is planning a new wave of canonisations which include English Cardinals Newman and Manning as well as Pope Pius XII and John XXIII.

Martyrs or Traitors?

The distinction that Christians seek to make between Protestant and Catholic martyrs is best seen through the perspective that history provides. In a previous chapter mention has been made of those in the mission field today, as throughout Christian history, who unacknowledged and unsung are being martyred for the truth. In contrast the media has given much coverage to the 'martyrdom' of the six Jesuit priests of El Salvador, who unquestionably were caught up in the political process at the time of their deaths.

At the time of the extensive press coverage of the 1987 beatification of 85 'English martyrs', the London-based United Protestant Council put out a well researched release, part of which is reproduced here. It went out to all the national newspapers, but nothing was printed in any of them.

'No one who is concerned for historical truth can be satisfied with the claim, by the Church of Rome, that the 85 English subjects that have been 'beatified' by the Pope were martyrs, which means that they suffered for their faith alone. The 288 martyrs who were put to death during Mary I's five year reign suffered solely for their faith. They were condemned on purely religious charges, being principally that they refused the doctrine of transubstantiation, which is the belief that the bread and wine in the mass are changed into the actual body and blood of Christ. They never denied that Mary was the lawful Queen of England, nor maintained any of her open and foreign enemies, nor procured any rebellion or civil war. They did not sow sedition in secret places, nor withdraw any subjects from their obedience.

Such charges of treason, however, were legitimately brought against those Roman Catholics who were put to death under the reign of Elizabeth and succeeding monarchs, and whose names are included in the recent list of those' beatified' by the Pope in Rome. ...

No Roman Catholic was executed in the first eleven years of Elizabeth I's reign, prior to the Pope Pius V inciting all Roman Catholics to rebellion, commanding them not to obey her, on pain of excommunication. It is an unchallengeable fact that no Roman Catholic was executed solely on account of his religious beliefs. The truth is that most of those laymen 'beatified' were put to death for assisting the 'seminary priests' in their design to bring down the throne; 63 out of the 85 'English martyrs' were 'seminary priests', trained abroad and sent back to further the plots of the Pope to undermine the English throne. These had been stepped up after Pope Gregory VII's sanctioning of the assassination of Elizabeth in 1580 and the organising of invasion in 1588. ...

With this background in mind it is impossible to agree that these men were martyrs in any proper sense of the word. On the contrary, what the Church of Rome is engaged in doing is glorifying traitors, spies and conspirators.'

History Rewritten

The same protest had been made over the 1970 canonisation of *'Forty Martyrs of England and Wales'* by Pope Paul VI. On that occasion the 'Saints' had included Thomas Garnett and Nicholas Owen, two of the conspirators in the notorious Gunpowder Plot of 1605.

With Protestantism on the ropes, the process of rewriting the history of our country is gathering pace. The *Discovery Pack*, marketed by Marshall Cavendish, first sold to millions of young people in 1988, and since then remarketed as a game, portrays Guy Fawkes as the young idealist, unswervingly loyal to the Roman Catholic faith, who endured persecution at the hands of his accusers. He too may well be beatified, or even canonized, before long. A cryptic letter to the *Daily Telegraph* on 1st November, 1989, from J.G.Lynch of Midlothian, headed 'burning insult', asked if the BBC had added a new feast to the church calendar. 'After *Songs of Praise* on 29th October (1990), we were invited to join in again next Sunday in *Songs of Praise for Bonfire Night*: St Guy Fawkes?'

The canonisation of Thomas Henry Garnet as one of the '*Forty Martyrs*' illustrates perhaps better than anything just how far things have gone in our lifetime. The Gunpowder Plot was a Jesuit conspiracy to blow up King and Parliament, which was to lead to an armed rising against the Monarchy. Garnet, who was Superior of the Jesuits in England at that time confessed to his guilt, and was hanged for his participation in this most terrible of crimes. His confession, written in his own hand, is still preserved in the Public Record Office: (SP 14/20, 4th April, 1605: PRO)

'I, Henry Garnet, of the Society of Jesus, priest, do freely confess before God that I hold the late intention of the Powder action to have been altogether unlawful and most horrible; as well in respect of the injury and treason to his Majesty, the Prince, and others that should have been sinfully murdered at that time; as also in respect of infinite other innocents which should have been present. ... I do acknowledge myself highly guilty, to have offended God, the King's Majesty and Estate, and humbly ask of all forgiveness; exhorting all Catholics whatsoever, that they in no way build on my example; but by prayer and otherwise seek the peace of the Realm, hoping in his Majesty's merciful disposition that they shall enjoy their wonted quietness and not bear the burden of mine or others' defaults and crimes. In testimony hereof I have written this with my own hand, 4th April, 1605'

The portrait of Henry Garnet, 'Saint and Martyr' of the Roman Catholic faith, certainly until recently, has for a long time been hanging in the hall of the Jesuit's College in Rome.

Also recently canonized among the 'Forty Martyrs' was Jesuit Edmund Campion, who in 1580 was found guilty of 'conspiracy to depose and kill the Queen; to cause war, slaughter and insurrection and to change religion and government; and to call in foreign armies.' He was executed for these crimes. Campion was canonised in 1970 by Pope Paul VI.

Another controversial canonisation was that of Thomas More back in 1935. He was established as a heroic figure in the public mind by influential Catholic writers such as Hilaire Belloc and Evelyn Waugh, as well as by G.K. Chesterton, who described him as 'the greatest historical character in English history.' His portrayal by Robert Bolt in the film *A Man For All Seasons*, firmly established More as one of the great men of faith of his time or of any other time. But this is fantasy, not history. In his well known 1982 book *The Statesman and the Fanatic*, historical author, Jasper Ridley, reveals More as a fanatic, and one 'who stood for the opposite of everything that he is admired for today ... He may not have flogged heretics in his garden, but there was nothing that More more strongly disapproved of than freedom, individual conscience, and religious toleration.'

In fact 'heretics'[2] were flogged in his garden. Wylie's *History of Protestantism* and Fox's *Acts and Monuments* or 'Book of Martyrs', immensely important reading for Christians today, describe the scourging and torture of 'those guilty of studying the Scriptures', and 'holding purely Protestant doctrines,' including John Tewkesbury, a trader and James Bainham, a lawyer, at the 'Tree of Truth' in Sir Thomas More's garden.

On 24th January, 1935 the Protestant Truth Society sent the following telegram to Pope Pius XI, who was at that time presiding over the Canonization Council, justifying the raising to sainthood of Sir Thomas More and Bishop John Fisher;

---

[2] The use of the word 'heretic', without the inverted commas, referring to true Christians, is typical of our time. The Oxford Dictionary of the Christian Church, under the heading 'Smithfield' has this short and dismissive entry; 'The place, in London, noted formerly as the site of executions, esp. during the Reformation period, when in the "fires of Smithfield" during Mary Tudor's reign about 300 heretics were burned there. It is now famous as a meat market.'

'Vienna, Charles V and Henry VIII State Papers, 27th September, 1533, disclose Bishop Fisher a traitor, planning Spanish invasion of England. Shall we send copies of State Papers before you proceed further with the Canonisation on 29th January ?'

After some courteous correspondence in which the Vatican received photo-copies of the Papers made by the British Public Record Office, the facts were sent to the Press Association. Only two newspapers published them – *The Daily Herald* and *The News Chronicle*. It is interesting to notice that neither of these two newspapers is published today. (*Jesuit Plots from Elizabethan to Modern Times*: A. Close: Wycliffe Press 1988)

The First Ecumenical Saint – J.H. Newman

With characteristic fine timing the cause for sainthood of Cardinal John Henry Newman was presented to the Pope in July 1989 even as an Anglo-Catholic campaign to make him an Anglican Saint gathered momentum in the centenary of his death. Clifford Longley's opinion in *The Times* that 'Newman certainly wrote the agenda of the Second Vatican Council from the grave,' has had backing from more than one Pope, by whom he has been credited with inspiring what is often called 'Newman's Council.' Newman's cause for Sainthood has been getting 'top priority' at the Vatican, according to his Postulator, Jesuit Father Vincent Blehl. He has already been pronounced 'venerable', the first stage of the three part process. He does still lack a physical miracle accredited to him, normally needed for the second stage of 'beatification', but the Pope is expected to make an exception because of 'the moral miracle of his exceptional spiritual influence.'

John Henry Newman, whose reputation is growing rapidly in the climate of unity, seems certain to emerge as the first Ecumenical Saint. The centenary of his death, in 1990, was commemorated and his life celebrated by the Church and given a great deal of media coverage. Thomas Cranmer's quincentenary, by comparison, made little

Roman Catholic Cardinal Basil Hume and the Archbishop of Canterbury Dr Robert Runcie at the service marking the 25th anniversary of a Vatican decree on Christian unity.
© The Press Association, January 1990

impact on the nation. Newman is particularly remembered for his attempt to reconcile *The Council of Trent* with *The Thirty Nine Articles* of the Church of England. Cranmer, author of the Thirty Nine Articles, devoted his life to highlighting the differences between the teaching of Rome and the Biblical doctrine of the National Church. As Director of the Church of England's *Church Society*, David Samuel, said at that time: 'It is not at all surprising therefore that the former should be as much feted as the latter neglected.'

Newman, whose 'reformulation of doctrine' was particularly praised by former Archbishop of Canterbury, Robert Runcie, believed that developing doctrine is really synonymous with continuing revelation, a view shared in many strands of Charismatic and Liberal thought today. Dr Runcie expressed his belief that 'after conflicts, had come a miracle;' Newman had been the instrument in fashioning that miracle, and this meant that he was increasingly seen as a representative figure in the nineteenth century history of the Church.

Times have certainly changed. Nineteenth century statesman, William Gladstone, also a High Churchman, saw Newman's conversion to Rome as possibly the greatest religious crisis since the Reformation. Although now less visible, that crisis, of which the future Prime-Minister spoke, has deepened as 'reformulated doctrine' has spread and the ecumenical process has accelerated.

Certainly a considerable debt is owed to Newman's developing doctrine by those who helped put together the *Agreed Statements* of *ARCIC*. His *Essay on the Development of Christian Doctrine*, a uniquely ecumenical work, which he started as an Anglican and completed as a Roman Catholic, has been a proof text for all involved.

An examination of Newman's life and thought has been described by bemused Protestant scholars as an experience 'amid the encircling gloom,' but without the 'kindly light' to lead them. Such a reflection is not to make mockery of Newman's famous hymn, *Lead Kindly Light*, but to express something of what has been found among the output of a tortuous, complex and contradictory mind. One of his oldest friends, Dr Jelf, said that Newman's mind was always essentially Jesuitical; and fellow Roman Catholic Lord Acton described him as a 'manipulator of the truth.' As leader of the Tractarian Society, which was characterized by its secretivenes, he had defended what was called 'Economy in Teaching and Arguing,' setting out the truth advantageously or withholding it. Quoting Clement of Alexandria, Newman wrote: 'He both thinks and speaks the truth; except where careful treatment is necessary, and then as a physician for the good of his patients he will lie. ... 'nothing but the good of his neighbour will lead him to do this. He gives himself up for the Church.'

'Economy' was one term to describe this 'means to an end' doctrine of the Jesuits, 'Reserve' was another. The doctrine of 'Economy' or 'Reserve' was used to conceal much of the Ritualistic Movement of the nineteenth century, including the membership, objectives and activities of the Oxford Movement and Tractarian Society. Protestant 'watchman', Walter Walsh, has carefully researched all of this in his book, *The Secret History of the Oxford Movement*, which includes information about 'The Confraternity of the Blessed Sacrament', set up to re-introduce the doctrine of transubstantiation; 'The Guild of All Souls', to bring back purgatory and prayers for the dead; and 'The Order of Corporate Union', to plant the seeds of Ecumenical unity with Roman and Orthodox Churches.

Sainthood and the British Crown

When Newman became Britain's most famous convert to Rome in 1845, his confession prior to his confirmation was heard by George Spencer, known as Father Ignatius Spencer of St Paul, who also acted as his sponsor. Great great great uncle to Princess Diana, as well as great uncle to Sir Winston Churchill and convert to Rome in 1830 just before the start of the Oxford Movement, Fr Spencer is now in line for 'Sainthood'. The prominence of the publicity following the Vatican announcement of the cause's presentation speaks volumes about its significance. As Fr Jeremiah Donovan, like George Spencer a Passionist priest, told the *Sunday Telegraph* (*Sunday Telegraph* 14th

149

April, 1991): 'Rome will be keen to have a saint linked to the British Royal Family.' As is argued elsewhere in this book, this is surely an understatement. The canonisation is likely, like Newman's, to go through its three stages very quickly. The record for elevation to Sainthood is 352 days, achieved by St Anthony of Padua in the 13th century. Such speed would obviously draw attention to itself, but things are moving fast.

In his enthronement speech to the multi-faith congregation at Canterbury Cathedral on 19th April, 1991, Archbishop of Canterbury, George Carey, revealed his own strong ecumenical commitment in speaking of his predecessors as Archbishops who had been martyred for their faith.

He cited Alphege, Thomas Becket and William Laud, and omitted Thomas Cranmer. Alphege was a 10th century Benedictine monk; Becket and Laud in the 12th and 17th centuries both sought to bring the Church into the faith and practice, and under the authority, of Rome. Alphege and Becket are 'Saints' of the Roman Catholic Church; it may well be that Laud, the ritualist who persecuted Protestants, is destined to join them soon. Although George Carey's enthronement committed him to upholding the 39 Articles of Religion and the Book of Common Prayer, it is significant that among the martyrs of the faith that he cited he did not include the man most responsible for these principal formularies of the Anglican Church, Archbishop Thomas Cranmer.

Saint Thomas Becket and the National Church

The tomb of Thomas Becket in Canterbury Cathedral and the spiritual presence of this 'Saint' of the Roman Catholic Church in the principal Anglican Cathedral is proving to be important for the ecumenical movement. In 1982, Pope John Paul II and Archbishop Runcie prayed together at his shrine, and in 1989 Archbishop of York, John Habgood led pilgrims who had arrived for the first multi-faith gathering at the Cathedral into the shrine as their final destination. The three strands of this fully ecumenical pilgrimage had earlier converged at the place, another sacred site, where

Henry II had paid penance to the Pope following Becket's murder in 1170.

Anglo-Catholic T.S. Eliot's *Murder in the Cathedral*, in the same way as *A Man for All Seasons* (in respect of Thomas More), has greatly altered the public perception of what brought about the death of this Catholic hero of faith. Services are now held annually across the country on 29th December to commemorate Becket's 'martyrdom' with extensive coverage in the national media.

Becket's 'martyrdom', which stemmed from his preferred allegiance to the Papacy rather than the Crown, may well prove to be important in the near future in the revival of the principle that the State should not have power over the Church.

The great national debate, about what not long ago was the longest word of many a schoolboy, 'antidisestablishmentarianism,' is surfacing again in a new form. A number of trial balloons have been going up over the last few years and the British public has been prepared to seriously consider what was unthinkable less than a decade ago. At the beginning of 1989 the Bishop of Aston raised the question of the disestablishing of the Church of England just a year after *The Sunday Times* in its leader 'Modernise the Monarchy' had pointed out that; 'Ending the Protestant monopoly of the throne would not only be just; it would also free the Church of England of its cruel burden as the established church.' (*Sunday Times*: 31st January, 1988)

Such continuing speculation has led to a serious national discussion about Church and State, crown and mitre, in the wake of the 'Annus horribilis' of the royal family and the apparently irretrievable breakdown of the marriage of the heir to the throne. Archbishop of York, Dr John Habgood, appearing on BBC TV's *Heart of the Matter*, in January 1993, in a far from balanced programme apparently promoting disestablishment, raised the question of the Coronation Service; 'If this is to unify the nation, it must recognise that we now live in an ecumenical and multi-faith society,' he said. Archbishop of Canterbury, George Carey, was quick to endorse his deputy's view; 'The religious map of Britain has changed out of recognition and we have to look at that.' (*Daily Mail*: February 1st, 1993)

Constitutional experts believe that widening the scope of the Oath would effectively mean the disestablishing of the Church of England, as we now know it. As columnist and author, Paul Johnson, put it; 'there is no halfway house, no resting place, between having an Established Church and turning Britain into a secular society.' (*Daily Mail*: January 26, 1993)

With the Maastrict process also threatening the Protestant throne, the breath-taking speed in which these changes are taking place is seen by Christians as the withdrawal of the grace and blessing of God, the inevitable result of our national apostasy. The departure of the present royal family from their solemn oaths sworn to Almighty God, before the nation at the Accession, as well as to one another in Holy Matrimony, would seem, after forty years, to have reaped a whirlwind – much more than an 'annus horribilis'.

Her Majesty committed herself to upholding, to the utmost of her power, the statutes and laws of Scripture, 'the royal law' and the 'very oracles of God', as well as the Protestant Reformed Religion. During the forty years of her reign the royal assent has been given to legislation facilitating divorce, legalising abortion and homosexuality, and 'liberating' adultery and pornography.

The collapse of Prince Charles' marriage following his affair with Camilla, wife of Colonel Andrew Parker-Bowles, who is 'Silver-Stick in Waiting to Her Majesty the Queen', has helped to precipitate the constitutional crisis, and to encourage calls to change the Oath. Apart from taking advice on constitutional matters from Roman Catholic Lord St John of Fawsley, the royal family must have been influenced by their very close friendships with Roman Catholics in their attitude towards the Protestant vows which are sworn.

The Parker-Bowles family is Catholic, as is James Gilbey of the 'Dianagate' or 'Squidgy' telephone tape. Princess Diana, much influenced by her spiritual rapport with Mother Teresa and perhaps also with her 'favourite clairvoyant, Irish Roman Catholic psychic Betty Palko,' is 'taking instruction from a Dominican priest to convert to the Roman Catholic faith at a secret Oxford address,' reported the tabloid press (*Today*, 19th December, 1992 and *The People*, 27th December, 1992).

If these reports are true, the princess, once converted, may well ask the Pope for an annulment to her marriage, based on the infidelity of Prince Charles at the time of their Wedding and their exchange of vows. This would create a constitutional crisis that would very likely assist the ambitions of Rome.

Sir William Heseltine, Australian former private Secretary to the Queen, who was responsible for the 1969 BBC TV documentary that first lifted the veil behind which the royal family had traditionally hidden itself, has been Her Majesty's closest adviser for these matters for many years.

The 1st February, 1993 edition of the *Daily Telegraph* printed the Coronation Oath alongside news of the two Archbishops' recommendation for its revision. The Court Circular on that same day was mainly concerned with the representation of the Queen, the Duke of Edinburgh and their sons, the three royal princes, at the State Funeral of the former Govenor General of Canada – held at the *Mary Queen of the World Cathedral, Montreal*.

Chapter 14

Persecution and the Inquisition

Those who are in the battle to defend our Christian heritage are concerned by the Vatican's use of the media to make heroes out of villains, and its longstanding practice of canonising or beatifying those who for centuries have been widely regarded as persecutors of the true church. One long-standing example of this is St Dominic, who founded the Dominican Order, instituted the notorious Inquisition, and took on the primary responsibility for persecuting 'heretics,' i.e. Jews or Bible-believing Christians. Another in the same tradition is St Ignatius Loyola, whose Society of Jesus, an altogether more sophisticated organisation, was needed by the Vatican to take on the same role after the Reformation.

The present Pope proposed the canonization of Queen Isabella of Spain, in 1992, to coincide with the 500th anniversary of Columbus' voyage to the New World. Queen Isabella did launch the great explorer, but she also launched the Spanish Inquisition under Torquemada and expelled 200,000 Jews from Spain. Nevertheless Isabella's cause was represented at the Vatican as for 'one of the great Christians of history.' Protests from Muslims, however, large numbers of whom were also expelled by the fervent Queen, as well as from Jews, finally obliged the Vatican to reconsider.

In September 1987, it was intended that Fr Junipero Serra, the 18th century founder of the Californian Missions System and an active member of the Spanish Inquisition, be beatified during Pope John Paul II's 17th September, 1987 visit to Carmel near Monterey, California.

For two years leading up to the Papal visit, a commemorative United States 'Junipero Serra' postage stamp,[1] had been used by Americans for most international letters; and this together with other public relations activities had been used to prepare public opinion. However the indigenous Indians promised to protest and Chumash Indian leader, Cheq Weesh Auh-Ho-Oh, spoke to the media of 'Indian demonstrations like they have never seen before in all their lives.' He recalled the experience of the Serra 'Mission' when conversion was a brutal process; the Indian people were 'brought through baptism into slavery.' They were beaten with whips, chained in shackles and stocks, made to work the crops and construct mission buildings and they died like flies.

The American press reported that a Vatican spokesman had said that the Pope did not beatify Fr Serra, 'because of problems with timing and Vatican procedural requirements.' However, strangely, the *Catholic Herald* subsequently reported that the Pope did actually beatify Fr Serra during the visit. The press was so much preoccupied by his meeting with Clint Eastwood, the Mayor of Carmel; that perhaps for that reason they may not have covered the beatification. Given the declared strength of feeling against it, this was surely most helpful for the Vatican; an embarrassing protest was avoided and the Pope was thus able to describe Serra at the ceremony as 'a shining example of Christian virtue and missionary spirit, a defender and champion of the Indians.' (*Catholic Herald*, September 1987)

---

[1] The United States post office commemoration of Serra contrasts sharply with the decision of the British Post Office not to issue a commemorative stamp for the 500th anniversary of Thomas Cranmer's birth in 1989. Cranmer, who was Archbishop of Canterbury under three monarchs, was founder of the Church of England, joint-author of the Book of Common Prayer and, with Bishops Latimer and Ridley, a martyr of Christ at Oxford. The Post Office decision not to commemorate Cranmer's anniversary with a stamp issue, was presumably well-intentioned, to avoid offence and to assist ecumenical 'unity'; but , for all that, it amounts to a denial of the true history of our church and nation.

In December 1989, Pope John Paul II canonised the first Canadian-born Saint, Marie Margarite d'Youville, and praised the 'heroic charity' of her work among Montreal's poor. However, members of Montreal's black Catholic community expressed outrage at the canonisation, pointing out that St Marguerite inherited about a dozen slaves from her husband and allegedly bought and sold dozens of others.

There has been Jewish protest over the decision to canonise Edith Stein, who died at Auschwitz along with millions of others of Jewish origin. Catholic-convert Stein, known in the Roman Church as Sister Teresa Benedicta of the Cross, asked God to accept her life in atonement 'for the unbelief of the Jews'. She has already been beatified despite protests from the Jews, who feel the Pope is trying to cash in on the Holocaust. The other Catholic martyr of Auschwitz, Father Maximilian Kolbe, who is said to have given his life to have saved the father of three children, 'edited a horrible anti-semitic daily paper before the war,' according to *Observer* correspondent, Neil Ascherson. Kolbe has already been made a Saint of the Church of Rome. (*Observer*: Sunday 23 July, 1989)

Another Roman Empire

The Inquisition, led by the Dominicans and the Jesuits, was usually early on the scene following each territorial acquisition of the Spanish and Portuguese empires in the 16th and 17th centuries. The methods used, which all too often were similar to those used by Serra in California or the Nazi-backed Ustashis in Croatia, sowed the seeds of reaction and aversion that have proved to be a barrier for true missionaries ever since.

Albert Close, former Council Member of the *Protestant Truth Society*, writes of the Jesuit mission to Indonesia in 1559 that 'conversion was wonderfully shortened by the co-operation of the colonial governors whose militia offered the natives the choice of the musket ball or of baptism. It was this type of Christianity which the Chinese government ignored in 1913 when it requested Protestant Britain and

North America to call on God Almighty to bless that great nation in the hour of her first birth of constitutional government. They ignored the Pope, because they did not regard Romanism as Christianity in any shape or form. The Chinese judged the missionaries and their teachings by their fruits.' (*The Divine Programme of the World's History*: A. Close)

In Japan, following the activities of the Roman Catholic 'missionaries', which culminated in 'the setting on foot of a Catholic army of 30,000 Japanese, which marched against the civil and military representatives of the Japanese government,' the *Exclusion Edict* of 1639 was introduced: 'For the future, let none, so long as the Sun illuminates the World, presume to sail to Japan, not even in the quality of ambassadors, and this declaration is never to be revoked, on pain of death.'

Given all that we have been looking at, it is instructive just to consider this statement alongside the exclusion clauses in the Bill of Rights which was enacted in England just 50 years afterwards.

Japan had thrown open her doors eagerly when Western navigators and explorers had first arrived. Now they were firmly closed and she retreated again into feudal isolationism. Following the experience with Vatican imperialism, she became convinced that Christianity represented nothing but a 'torturous Western device for political and religious domination.' (Avro Manhattan: *Vietnam, Why Did We Go?*) Since then and right up to the post-war period, the Japanese, a people, with long memories, very much conditioned by their history and steeped in ancestor-worship, have been deeply suspicious of 'Christians'. It is not surprising therefore that Japan is the least evangelised major nation on earth today.

This does also perhaps help to explain the cruelty and savagery of Japanese atrocities in the Pacific War, although of course it does not excuse them.

'Vatican plans to turn 1992 into a triumphal celebration of 500 years of discovery and evangelisation in Latin America are beginning to backfire', wrote Jan Rocha in *The Guardian* in April 1991; 'as indigenous groups meet to denounce the Catholic Church's role in the genocide which they say "discovery" brought for them. "To celebrate the 500 years is to celebrate a massacre", said Indian leaders in Mexico. In Ecuador they concluded that what had happened was "an invasion which brought genocide through the contagion with European diseases, exploitation and the separation of parents and children." In Peru, the South American Indigenous Council went further, saying: "If observers from international human rights organisations had been present during the invasion and the immediate years afterwards, then the Spanish State and the Catholic Church would have been universally condemned for their atrocities against the Indian peoples. The genocide perpetrated against the Indians makes Hitler's genocide against the Jews seem a minor deed."' (*The Guardian*: International News Section, April 20 1991)

Twentieth Century Inquisition – Croatia

We don't need to go back so far in history to catch another glimpse of this same 'evangelising spirit'. According to a memorandum in the United States Army's Counter Intelligence Corps documents, dated 12th September, 1947, agents hunting escaped Nazi war criminals after World War II purposely avoided capturing one man, because; 'his contacts are so high and his present position so compromising to the Vatican, that any extradition of the Subject would deal a staggering blow to the Roman Catholic Church'. (*Battle Cry*: Chick Publications, Chino, California)

The man was Anton Pavelic, head of the new nation state of Croatia, carved out of Yugoslavia during the War. During Pavelic's four-year reign, he and Roman Catholic Prelate, Archbishop Alois Stepinac, pursued a 'convert or die' policy among the 900,000 Greek Othodox Serbs, Jews and others in Croatia. 200,000 were converted; 700,000, who chose to die, were tortured, burned, buried alive or shot, after digging their own graves. This appalling persecution carried out by the Ustashis included many of the worst atrocities of the War; certainly the mutilations were horrific, the savagery terrible.

The Catholic Church did not leave the execution of a religious war to the secular arm. She was there herself, openly, ignoring precautions and bolder than she had been for a very long time. Wielding the hatchet or dagger, pulling the trigger, organising the massacre, the Roman Catholic Priesthood became again its own instrument of inquisition, as in the days of Torquemada. Many of the Ustashi officers were priests or friars sworn to fight 'with dagger or gun', for the 'triumph of Christ and Croatia'. (Avro Manhattan: *The Vatican's Holocaust*, Ozark Books, Springfield, MO, 1986) Priests played a prominent role in the closing or takeover of Orthodox churches, the seizure of church records and the interrogation of the Orthodox clergy. They also supervised concentration camps and organised the torture of many of the victims. French author, Edmond Paris, who was born a Roman Catholic and has written a very thorough account of this terrible massacre, *Convert or Die*, has said; 'It is difficult for the world to believe that a whole people could be doomed to extermination by a government and religious hierarchy of the twentieth century, just because it happened to belong to another ethnical and racial group and had inherited the Christianity of Byzantium rather than that of Rome.' (Edmond Paris: *Convert or Die*: Chick Publications, Chino, CA). The world doesn't in fact know and is thus unable to understand fully what has happened in Yugoslavia in 1991.

Writing in September 1991, *Sunday Telegraph* writer Andrew Roberts expressed surprise that 'in the present crisis, almost the entire Western media have chosen to champion the Croats.' He goes on to ask the question; 'how are the Serbs expected to react to the decision to adopt the Ustashi's chequered symbol as the Croatian national flag? In Krajina it takes longer than the 45 minute attention span of today's CNN broadcaster to forget the way Franciscan friars participated in the slaughter of Serbs in Croatian Bosnia. Orthodox Serbs were promised protection if they converted to Catholicism and were then killed after they entered the churches, as the priests looked on.' (*Sunday Telegraph:* 15th September 1991)

In his authoritative book *Roman Catholicism*, Professor

Loraine Boettner records his own reaction to such enormous crimes being covered up at the time and since; 'Most astonishing was the manner in which those crimes were ignored or hushed up at the time by almost all news services, although similar massacres of Jews in Germany were given the widest publicity – another demonstration of how subtly and efficiently Roman clericalism exerts its influence over the press and radio. But now a French author, who was born a Roman Catholic, has told the story in his fully documented books, *The Vatican against Europe* and *Genocide in Satellite Croatia*. Another French author, Herve Lauriere, also a Roman Catholic by birth, has recorded the same events in his *Assassins in the Name of God*. Both Paris and Lauriere put the responsibility squarely on the priests of the Church of Rome.' (*Roman Catholicism*: Loraine Boettner, Banner of Truth, 1962)

The attempt to create the entirely Roman Catholic Independent State of Croatia was accompanied by a persecution so ferocious that it is difficult to find a parallel in all of history. In the Spanish Inquisition under Torquemada, some 125,000 people perished by burning, torture and hunger. The St Bartholomew Massacre, in France, in 1572, accounted for 100,000 victims. But the inquisition of the Serbian Orthodox by the Croatian Catholics was more terrible and on a much bigger scale, with 750,000 Serbs killed in just four years.

p158 ← Pavelic's crimes were covered up by the Vatican's top-level contacts among the Allied Powers and he was allowed to join many other Roman Catholic war criminals who were spirited out of Europe through the Roman Church's 'monastery escape route'. This 'Rat Line' was managed by a Croatian clergyman in association with the Vatican, according to the September 1991 Obituary written for Klaus Barbie in the *Independent*. (*The Independent*: 27th September 1991) In 1959, Pavelic returned from Argentina and Chile for medical treatment in a German hospital in Madrid. On the day he died a few months later, his personal benediction was given by Pope John XXIII. His collaborator in these unspeakable crimes, Alois Stepinac, was made a Cardinal by Pope Pius XII after the war, although

160

he was arrested in 1946 and sentenced to life imprisonment by the Tito regime. Stepinac had twice visited Pius XII, in Rome, in 1942, reporting on the 'conversions' of 244,000 Serbs to Roman Catholicism. His death in 1960 aroused a powerfully orchestrated concert of lamentation and praise in every Catholic country. He had been treated like a martyr in Roman Catholic circles because he had been held for five years under house arrest. Cardinal Spellman in New York even named a parochial high school after him. The man who wrote, in 1941, 'Hitler has been sent by God,' and who wrote in a pastoral letter that what was being done in Croatia by the Ustashi regime was 'the Lord's work', will, hereafter, wear a halo and be canonised, predicted Edmond Paris. (*Ustashi in a Free World*: Edmond Paris, Convert or Die, Chick Publications, California).

Stepinac's successor, Cardinal Franjo Kuharic is pressing the Yugoslav State to revoke the sentence as a prelude to Stepinac's canonization, according to the *Independent* newspaper of November 1990.

There is great concern that Croatian nationalism powered once more by that same religious spirit, is rising again, although what the Serbs see as their pre-emptive military action in neighbouring Bosnia Herzgovina will deter it.

Medjugorje is a Croat village in Herzegovina. The seventeen million pilgrims said to have visited the Marian shrine there during the past nine years are mostly unaware that the Franciscans who run the church and champion the visionaries are passionate nationalists, who even claim that the Virgin speaks 'pure Croat', rather than Serbo-Croat, as most Yugoslavs still call their language. The most extreme Croat nationalists have been to, or hope to go to, Medjugorje. Pictures of Medjugorje Church and the statue of Mary often appear among nationalistic manifestations, and are propped up against the cathedral walls during Mass. (Richard West: 'Brother Devil's Legacy', *The Independent Magazine*, 10th November, 1990)

The square in front of that same cathedral in Zagreb, capital of Croatia, is to be named after Cardinal Alois Stepinac, forty years after he was imprisoned for what are now described only as his 'alleged' crimes. 'He is a great hero in our country and widely admired for his courage,' said Mr Miejenko Zagar, General Secretary of the new ruling Christian Democratic Union. (*The Universe*: 4th November, 1990) Croat National Guardsmen pray at the tomb of the man who nearly fifty years before on Easter Day 1941, from the pulpit in Zagreb Cathedral, had announced the illegal establishment of the Independent State of Croatia. and had backed and made respectable the most ruthless, cruel and barbaric regime that quite possibly the world has ever known.

The Modern Inquisition

The rehabilitation of the Inquisition of old is something of an article of faith for the Vatican; for the Inquisition is alive and well and, within the restrictive limits placed on it by democratic freedoms, as powerful as ever. Roman Catholic author, theologian and former priest, Peter de Rosa, in his 1988 book *Vicars of Christ, the Dark Side of the Papacy*, writes about the modern Inquisition; '...located at "Casa Santa", the Pope's house on the corner is known locally as the Palace of the Inquisition. In recent years, having had a bad press, the Holy, Catholic and Apostolic Inquisition, like the Soviet secret police, had been renamed more than once. In 1908, this oldest of Rome's Sacred Congregations, became *The Holy Office*. From 1967, it changed to the *Congregation for the Doctrine of the Faith*. The present Secretary and Chief Executive, the Grand Inquisitor of Old, is the Bavarian Cardinal Ratzinger, but the President has ever been the reigning Pontiff.'

Elsewhere Professor de Rosa describes Ratzinger, 'the Pope's right-hand man', 'picking up the 'phone and calling a priest in Los Angeles, telling him either to suppress his researches into the views of bishops on celibacy, or to pack his bags and leave within the hour. It is not surprising that theologians are removed from their teaching posts, priests are suspended from office for opposing non-infallible teaching. It is not surprising that a Bishop is disciplined for acting as Jesus acted, ministering to the downcast, refusing to

162

excommunicate anyone who has sincerity or love in his heart.'

It is this same Cardinal Ratzinger who has pronounced on *ARCIC* and ecumenical progress, seeking more concessions on the doctrine of salvation and the role of the Church. (*Observations*: Congregation for the Doctrine of the Faith, January 1989).

In the high-profile Vatican of the last years of the millennium, the Cardinal's public image is important too. According to *The Catholic Herald*, 'Austere Cardinal Joseph Ratzinger, dubbed in Italy the latter day inquisitor, for his Doctrinaire Guidance as prefect of the Congregation for the Doctrine of the Faith, is tipped to become the star-turn of a new Italian TV station.' The article says that the Vatican strongly denies financing it, and the initial cash was provided by two Roman *Opus Dei* businessmen. (*Catholic Herald*, 13th January, 1989)

Chapter 15

Concern of Roman Catholics

Concern about the direction of the Papacy has been voiced by many within the Roman Church. Foremost critic of John Paul's pontificate among Catholic prelates was traditionalist Archbishop Marcel Lefebvre, who died in March 1991, aged 85. Lefebvre, who was excommunicated in 1988 for consecrating bishops into his society, named after the conservative Pope Pius X, complained that the Polish Pontiff, 'speaks all the time about the rights of man, about ecumenism, not about truth.' (*Catholic Herald*: 29th March, 1991)

Peter de Rosa, author of *Vicars of Christ, the Dark Side of the Papacy* and Piers Compton, author of *The Broken Cross*, both committed Roman Catholics, wrote the books from which we have quoted, out of their concern for the Church of Rome which each of them from a different perspective sees as being in great danger. They represent two entirely different positions within Roman Catholicism. On the one hand, Professor de Rosa is opposed to what he sees as the doctrinaire, autocratic and backward-looking nature of the papacy under John Paul, which for him contrasts very unfavourably with the progressive and compassionate pontificate of John XXIII.

Compton, on the other hand, was deeply concerned by the liberal departures of Vatican II and the accompanying disregard of ancient and hallowed tradition and orthodoxy. This view which is represented most strongly by the ultra-conservative wing of the Roman Church led by Archbishop Lefebvre, underlines the fact that the Ecumenical initiative launched by Vatican II is by no means carrying all Catholics with it. This certainly applies to Anglo-Catholics too; and the formation of the 'High Church' group, *Church in Danger*, is an expression of their unwillingness to be swept along with the 'lowest common denominator'.

The Roman Church is extraordinary in its ability to face both ways at the same time, while appearing to be firm and clear. The John Paul II Papacy displays this as much as any previous pontificate. Although widely perceived to be both conservative and orthodox, this Pope, according to Dr Malachi Martin who worked closely with him; 'can still cause devout Catholics to question the legitimacy of a Pontiff who has made a conscious decision to allow the Roman Catholic Church to fester into corruption, Masonry, satanic pedeophilia, and outrageous disobedience on the part of the clergy and laity.' (*The Keys of This Blood*: Malachi Martin, review by *NRI Trumpet*; Aurora, Colorado)

Dr Martin, who in spite of this observation, generally appears sympathetic towards Pope John Paul and evidently believes in his inspired mission, argues that dicipline and Papal authority have broken down in the Church and that the Pope has permitted this, pending that sign from the Heavens, promised by Our Lady of Fatima, which will herald John Paul's assumption of moral and spiritual leadership over the whole world. The sign in the sky, which the Pope is convinced will be manifested soon, is accompanied by the 'second coming of Mary', predicted by the first apparition at Fatima.

There clearly is a disciplinary problem in the Roman Church, with considerable resistance on both the conservative and liberal wings to the Pope's policies, especially among the Church's leading thinkers. As with the finances, an impression may sometimes be given that matters are getting out of control. However the great majority of Roman Catholics remain unswervingly loyal to the Pontiff and to the authority of the Vatican; and the discipline of the whole institution is perceived by the public at large, at least, to remain as solid as ever. The unequivocal positions apparently adopted by the present Pope, his firmness with liberal theologians, his strong moral stance, all go down well with committed Catholics and, significantly, with many Evangelicals too. The Anglo-Catholic newsletter, *Ecclesia*, noted in December 1990 that 'the present Pope is doing a great deal to return his Church to better ways after the appalling mess caused by the "spirit" of Vatican II.' (*Universe*: 16th December, 1990)

Quite how John Paul II manages to retain the allegiance of serious Catholics while, in step with the utterances of the Madonna of Medjugorje, he embraces other faiths, is beyond rational understanding.

Chapter 16

Sounding the Alarm

'No right minded Protestant could place his trust in the promises of the Vatican. A Church for all seasons; 'Semper Eadem', but adaptable, compliant and blending into her surrounds, she adopts the cause which will win her ascendancy. These are her politics and her diplomacy and this is her ecumenism.' (*Catholic Research Information Bureau*, 1987)

The Roman Church is frequently described in Protestant literature as 'a lamb in adversity, a fox when in equality, and a tiger when in the ascendancy.'

Prime Minister W.E. Gladstone had sounded a strong warning to posterity about the designs of this great institution. In 1874 and just four years after Rome had lost her territorial possessions, he wrote: 'Individual servitude, however abject, will not satisfy the Latin church. The State must also be a slave.' Gladstone, leader of the British Empire at the height of its global power and influence, was well placed to recognise papal ambitions.

So also were Prime Ministers Sir Robert Peel and Benjamin Disraeli. Peel had predicted after the 1829 *Emancipation Act* that equality would not be enough and that the Roman Church would be satisfied by nothing but ascendancy. Disraeli, later in the century, saw it clearly enough; 'Your empire and your liberties are more in danger at this moment than when Napoleon's army of observation was encamped at Boulogne,' he observed.

Bismarck's experience in Europe was no different. 'The Papacy', said Prince Bismarck, 'has ever been a political power which, with the greatest audacity and with the most momentous consequences, has interfered in the affairs of this world.'

Earlier in the nineteenth century historian Lord Macaulay had written; 'The experience of 1200 eventful years, the ingenuity and patient care of forty generations of statesmen have improved the polity of the Church of Rome to such perfection, that among the contrivances which have been devised for deceiving and controlling mankind, it occupies the highest place.'

In the 17th Century, philosopher Thomas Hobbes had identified this polity in his famous description of the Roman Church; 'the Papacy is no other than the ghost of the deceased Roman Empire, sitting crowned upon the grave thereof.'

Adam Smith, in his *Wealth of Nations*, also added his warning for posterity: 'The constitution of the Church of Rome may be considered the most formidable combination that was ever formed against the authority and security of civil government, as well as against the liberty, reason and happiness of mankind.'

Those who are sounding the alarm today seek to show that ecumenism is the up-to-date 'contrivance for deceiving and controlling mankind.' The Catholic Church's 'pragmatic' attitude to ecumenism and the 'separated brethren', at home and abroad, is very well illustrated by a *Daily Telegraph* article on Pope John Paul II's visit to La Paz, Bolivia in April 1987. Speaking to the meeting of 39 Catholic bishops, of whom only 12 were native Bolivians, the Pope warned against the 'proselytising activities of sects which have multiplied recently in Bolivia; these so called Fundamentalist sects, which are sowing confusion.' There is no doubt his remarks referred to Bible believing Christians.

In Ireland the Roman Catholic Church has not joined in with the new ecumenical structure, but retained observer status. When the Roman Church is in the minority, as she is in Britain, her policy has ever been to join in and seek to control and absorb those with whom she has made common cause. When she is in the majority, as she in in Ireland, she is quite different. She holds herself aloof and seeks to demolish those who disagree with her.

But Rome has been reassuring about her intentions. According to Cardinal Suenens: 'The Second Vatican Council closed the age of Counter-Reformation. Obviously the climate has not done away with real doctrinal differences and there are some who say, 'The glaciers may melt, but the Alps will remain.' We cannot share this pessimistic view. Even now, men are digging into the sides of the mountain challenging its resistance and preparing tunnels.'

The Cardinal was careful to deal with accusations and suspicions about spiritual and temporal domination: 'There is nothing that will free the Papacy more completely from all suspicions of absolutism and authoritarianism than the application in daily life of 'primacy of service', which will be more effective than doctrinal discussion.' 'Without temporal power, the church of Vatican II has but one ambition, to aid the world in freeing men from ignorance, mistrust and fratricidal hatred, and to aid the building of the humanism of tomorrow, combining all the power of the forces of peace.'

Billy Graham

Many evangelical leaders today share Cardinal Suenens' ecumenical optimism. Billy Graham felt J.F. Kennedy's election as President had 'helped relations between the churches and created a better understanding between Protestant and Catholic churches in America.' When Graham was conversing with Cardinal Cushing on network TV in October, 1964, Cushing said to him: 'You've made a great contribution to the Ecumenical spirit because you've tossed a banner bearing the fact that Christians agree on more things than they disagree on.'

More recently, Billy Graham has gone further in endorsing and contributing to the ecumenical process. In 1979 he expressed to the Associated Press his hope that Pope John Paul's visit to the United States will launch a new wave of spiritual revival.' Those who 'received Christ' at the Billy Graham crusades, at which so many in the past found Christ, were told to go back to their churches. Roman Catholics who come forward in response to the message are handed over to the local clergy of the Church of Rome for follow up. This has been the standard practice of the Billy Graham Association for many years.

In January 1981 Billy Graham described the Pope as 'the greatest moral leader of the world and the world's greatest evangelist.' Dr Graham's enthusiasm for close working with Roman Catholicism has been a very influential factor in the advance of ecumenical unity in the 80's.

Friend and confidante to every United States President since Harry Truman and spiritual counsel to a number of them, including George Bush today, Billy Graham is regularly featured in *Time* magazine's 'top ten most respected men'. He is conspicuously careful not to cause offence or to adopt controversial positions which might forfeit his close relationship with kings and political leaders, or his near universal popularity. For example, when asked by the BBC radio programme *Sunday* about Nancy Reagan's consultation of an astrologer in relation to President Reagan's diary, Dr Graham replied, 'Astrology is all right as long as it is not taken too seriously.' He surely knows better; for 'the Bible says' ... otherwise. The Scripture makes very clear the source of the spirit behind astrology, that it is forbidden by God, and that those who practise it are heading for damnation. (Isaiah 47:14)

The Apostle Paul certainly could not have spoken more clearly to us about this kind of compromise:

> '... Or do I seek to please men? for if I yet pleased men, I should not be the servant of Christ.'   Galatians 1:10

Yet when Billy Graham began his ministry as an itinerant evangelist, he proclaimed that the three greatest dangers facing the world were Islam, Roman Catholicism and Communism. In more than 40 years, he has moved a long way from this position. Having been given tremendous publicity by the Roman Catholic media baron, William Randolph Hearst and his powerful group of newspapers, and later on having accepted an honorary doctorate from a

Jesuit seminary, he clearly departed from the distinctive evangelical stance with which he began. In 1972, he received the Catholic International Franciscan Award for 'his contribution to true ecumenism.'

The Welsh publication, *Rallying Cry*, summarized what had taken place: 'The tragic decline of this Christian hero is exposed; one which began way back in 1954. Then, or even earlier, he let go his love for Christian doctrine and a desire to contend for it, in favour of a more popular appeal. No doubt, American Big Business behind the Billy Graham Evangelistic Organisation argued against the narrow view which a doctrinal appreciation would give him. In Big Business, success means riding high upon tidal waves of popularity. Thus, Billy Graham was obliged to reach out beyond the limited confines of God's sheepfolds, to the wider acres where goats graze and wolves prey!'

President of *The Evangelical Theological Society*, Dr Richard Pierard, described Billy Graham as the 'chief force in promoting ecumenism among evangelicals.' American Bible Teacher, Dr Charles Woodbridge said much the same in a solemn warning to the evangelist: 'If you persist in making common cause with those that deny the Word of God, and thus in minimizing the sharp line of distinction between those that are loyal and those who are disloyal to the Scriptures, it is my strong opinion that you will be known as the great divider of the church of Christ of the 20th century.'

'Mark them which cause divisions and offences contrary to the doctrine that you have learned; and avoid them.'
Romans 16:17 & 18

In an interview with *US News and World Report* in December 1988, Dr Graham said: 'World travel and getting to know the clergy of all denominations has helped mould me into an ecumenical being. We're separated by theology and, in some instances by culture and race, but all of that means nothing to me any more.' (*US News and World Report*: 19th December, 1988)

He paved the way for diplomatic relations between the

United States and the Vatican, something that had never happened before. (*Charisma magazine*: May 1984, pages 101 & 102). A letter by Billy Graham sent to President Reagan's National Security Adviser, William P. Clark, was quoted in the *Chicago Sun Times* as saying: 'If anyone can do it and get away with it, it is Mr Reagan ...'

The famous evangelist's visits to Russia and East European countries had the approval, backing and diplomatic enhancement of the Vatican, and thus it is not surprising to learn that those behind the Iron Curtain whom the Pope and former Archbishop Runcie have described as 'fundamentalists', felt betrayed by Billy Graham's apparent accommodation of Communism and his disavowal of their plight during those visits. Before his July 1989 mission to Hungary, three Protestant pastors called on him to repent for collaborating with oppressive dictatorships in Eastern Europe. In an open letter dated 20th April, 1989, Gyozo Dobner, Gabor Ivanyi and Geza Nemeth expressed sadness that on previous visits to Eastern Europe, especially to Romania in 1985, Billy Graham was 'manipulated by dark powers.' He was quoted as saying that the Ceausescu regime had 'resolved all nationality questions and guaranteed complete religious freedom for every religious community.' The three ministers noted that at that time it was well known that the country's leadership was causing 'immeasurable suffering ... and brutally violating human rights. The task of the faithful,' the pastors declared, 'is not to protect the oppressor, but to express unambiguously solidarity with the oppressed. The preaching of the gospel of Christ is incompatible with political falsehood.' (*Keston College News Service*)

Luis Palau is also working with Roman Catholics in his crusades and his 1987 New Zealand crusade was 'the first time the Catholic Church has ever backed a major evangelical mission.' (Australian *Challenge Weekly*, 18th April 1986).

Another View of Evangelism

Dr Martyn Lloyd-Jones was not one of those who could go along with this view of evangelism. In fact at the Second

National Assembly of Evangelicals in 1966, he parted company with other evangelical leaders including Jim Packer and John Stott over the issue of ecumenism. The First *NEAC Conference* at Keele the following year made public the gulf which had been opened up among evangelicals by this issue. Dr Lloyd-Jones spoke out boldly about the magnitude of the problem as he saw it. He told his congregation at Westminster Chapel:

> 'I remind you that the Protestant Reformers were not just bigoted zealots or fools. Their eyes were opened by the Holy Spirit; Luther, Calvin, Knox, all of them. They saw this horrible monstrosity depicted in the Bible and the warning against it. At the risk of even losing their lives they stood up and protested. They confronted Rome, ... The Roman Catholic Church is a counterfeit, a sham, it represents prostitution of the worst and most diabolical kind. It is indeed a form of the antichrist; it is to be rejected and denounced, but, above all, it is to be countered. And there is only one thing that can counter it and that is a Biblical, doctrinal Christianity. A Christianity that merely preaches "Come to Christ" or "Come to Jesus" cannot stand before Rome. Probably what that will do ultimately, will be to add to the numbers belonging to Rome. People who hold evangelistic campaigns and say, "Are you Roman Catholics? go back to your church," are denying New Testament teaching. We must warn them.' (*Bible League Quarterly October/December 1981*)

This sermon of Dr Lloyd-Jones was but an echo sounding down the centuries, of the bold and fearless exposition of The Word from the pulpit; sounds of the trumpet increasingly muted during this century.

Speaking in the 1880s, Dr H. Grattan Guinness sounded a strong clear note typical of his time;

> 'I see the great Apostacy, I see the desolation of Christendom, I see the smoking ruins, I see the reign of monsters; I see those vice-gods, that Gregory VII, that

Innocent III, that Boniface VIII, that Alexander VI, that Gregory XIII, that Pius IX; I see their long succession, I hear their insufferable blasphemies, I see their abominable lives; I see them worshipped by blinded generations, bestowing hollow benedictions, bartering lying indulgences, creating a paganized Christianity; I see their liveried slaves, their shaven priests, their celibate confessors; I see the infamous confessional , the ruined women, the murdered innocents; I hear the lying absolutions, the dying groans; I hear the cries of the victims; I hear the anathemas, the curses, the thunders of the interdicts; I see the racks, the dungeons, the stakes; I see that inhuman Inquisition, those fires of Smithfield, those butcheries of St Bartholomew, that Spanish Armada, those unspeakable dragonnades, that endless train of wars, that dreadful multitude of massacres. I see it all, and in the name of the ruin it has brought in the Church and in the world, in the name of the truth it has denied, the temple it has defiled, the God it has blasphemed, the souls it has destroyed; in the name of the millions it has deluded ; the millions it has slaughtered, the millions it has damned; with holy confessors, with noble reformers, with innumerable martyrs, with the saints of ages, I denounce it as the masterpiece of Satan, as the body and soul and essence of antichrist.' (*Romanism and the Reformation* by H. Grattan Guinness, DD: Focus Christian Ministries, Lewes, Sussex)

Charles Haddon Spurgeon, another gifted 19th century preacher, was every bit as firm about the true nature of Rome, and this had much to do with his parting of the ways with the Baptist Union:

'It is the bounden duty of every Christian to pray against Anti-Christ, and as to what Anti-Christ is no sane man ought to raise a question. If it be not the Popery in the Church of Rome there is nothing in the world that can be called by that name ... because it wounds Christ, because it robs Christ of His glory, because it puts sacramental efficacy in the place of His atonement, and lifts a piece of bread in the place of the Saviour, and a few drops of water in place of the Holy Ghost, and puts a fallible man like ourselves up as the Vicar of Christ on earth; if we pray against it, because it is against Him, we shall love the persons though we hate their errors; we shall love their souls though we loathe and detest their dogmas, and so the breath of our prayers will be sweetened, because we turn our faces towards Christ when we pray.'

With Billy Graham back in England in 1989, Free Presbyterian Church of Scotland's Clerk to the Synod, Revd Donald MacLean's comment in his letter to *The Times* 11th November, 1988 still deserves careful consideration;

'The Ecumenical movement which you praise is the greatest disaster to affect the Christian church this century. It has reduced the professing churches of this country to a collection of bloodless, spineless and boneless organisations, which can hardly raise a whimper on the side of Christ and His Truth. Small wonder that evil progresses as it does, and spiritual darkness becomes more intense as the years go by. You appear to regard a body of professing Christians, of sober conduct, and deep spirituality of mind, as fanatical and bigoted. If this be so then the eminent men of God, such as John Knox in Scotland, John Calvin and Martin Luther on the Continent, and Archbishop Cranmer in England were bigots in their contests with the errors of Popery. We are glad to be in such company.' (*The Times*: 9th November 1988)

The Baptist Confession of Faith, following on from the Westminster Confession, had its 300th anniversary commemorated in 1989. With wonderful clarity it expounds the great doctrines of grace and election, underlining the Lordship and Authority of Christ, and declares:

'that the Pope of Rome is that man of sin, and son of perdition, that exalteth himself in the church against Christ, and all that is called God; whom the Lord shall destroy with the brightness of His coming.'

Bishop J.C. Ryle, who stood strongly in the Protestant tradition, had no doubt about it:

'Unity without truth is useless. When Rome has repealed the decrees of Trent and her additions to the creed, and when she has formally renounced image worship, Mary worship, and transubstantiation, then and not until then, will it be time to talk of reunion with her. Till then I call on all Christians to resist to the death this idea of reunion with Rome.'

Chapter 17

The Pace of Ecumenical Progress

If the alarmists have it right, time is short. With the eyes of the Church of England on the very emotive but essentially secondary issue of the ordination of women, the 1988 Lambeth Conference voted almost unanimously to confirm the Swanwick Declaration of the previous year, and to abandon the Reformation and its solid foundations of faith. 1988 with all its anniversaries, reminding us of our great biblical heritage and of God's grace in preserving the nation from the tyranny of false religion, may well prove ironically to have been the year of decision for Protestantism and the Reformation in England.

Steps towards union of the Anglican and Roman Churches could follow very quickly now, although with such a whole-hearted consensus among Anglican leaders, the Vatican is understandably 'playing hard to get' and looking for a final agreement closer to its unchanging view. Agreement at the top cannot proceed faster than the consensus at the grassroots. Archbishop Runcie's acquiescence to the concept of Papal supremacy, and his enthusiastic announcement in Rome in September 1989 of the 'engagement' of the two churches with an intent to marriage brought a shocked reaction from many in both church and nation. There needs to be a pause at the national level.

There is no such pause at the local level. There, with the Inter-Church process and the Decade of Evangelism in full swing, the pace of ecumenical progress is breath-taking. Local covenants are being pledged and even signed all over the country with the Roman Catholic Church. Such covenants are contrary to the strong warning of Scripture:

'But above all things, my brethren, swear not, neither by heaven, neither by the earth, neither by any other oath: but let your yea be yea; and your nay, nay; lest ye fall into condemnation.'
James 5:12

A major instance was the signing of the Covenant for the Coalition on Revival in Washington DC in July 1986. The commitment to unity signed by such as Bob Mumford, John Wimber and Reconstructionists, Gary North and R.J. Rushdoony, provides for a non-quarrelling policy regarding doctrine, and declared principles for church leaders and thousands of congregations across America. A similar non-quarrelling policy guide is provided for the major conferences of the *International Charismatic Consultation on World Evangelisation*, including Brighton 91.

In towns like Coventry, Winchester and Guildford, *Churches Together* has united the great majority of the nation's churches for ecumenical covenants, special events, exchanges of preachers, services of mutual commitment, ecumenical missions and various youth activities. The sharing of churches by Anglicans and Roman Catholics, which has been going on for a number of years has been given fresh impetus by the Inter-Church Process. Respected Christian organisations such as Scripture Union and the United Bible Society have linked their names with the Ecumenical Instrument and involved themselves in ecumenical mission within the Decade of Evangelism and the Decade of Evangelisation. Inter-Church marriages, rare occurrences until twenty years ago and often featuring prominent Roman Catholics, have led to the forming of ecumenical groups and speeded up the ecumenical process. Inter-church communities are sharing monastic life, retreats and spiritual disciplines together. Pilgrimages to well-publicized ecumenical communities like Taize in France gain recognition in all quarters of the Church.

Milton Keynes, which styles itself 'the UK's first ecumenical city', appointed the nation's first Ecumenical Moderator on January 1st, 1991. Baptist minister, Hugh Cross, previously ecumenical officer for England became 'an ecumenical bishop in all but name'. The first ecumenical city built the first ecumenical church, 'Christ the Cornerstone', a £3 million domed edifice of 'cathedral proportions', which was dedicated by Her Majesty the Queen on March 13th, 1992.

'May this church in Milton Keynes be a pledge of our common commitment, a signpost to an increasingly shared future and a beacon of hope for the whole community,' said Roman Catholic Primate, Cardinal Hume, at the service of dedication. 'This would simply never have occurred to previous generations and demonstrates how far we are now committed to the work of Christian unity.'

The sermon preached to the Queen by the Cardinal, was another religious landmark (and again in breach of the Sovereign's Accession Oath) – the first sermon preached by a Roman Catholic to a reigning monarch, since the seventeenth century

'Semper Eadem', or a new Ecumenical Flexibility?

With such 'cooperation and commitment' being brought to bear, it is instructive to re-examine the basis for the new togetherness and its heady prospect of bringing the Gospel to all nations . Enthusiastic ecumenists may not all be aware of Cardinal Bea's definitive statement at Zurich in 1962; 'No concessions in dogma can be made by the Church for the sake of Christian unity. But pronouncements in many 'other areas' at the forthcoming Ecumenical Council (Vatican II) should make efforts towards unity easier.'

Presumably the pronouncements included among other things the replacement of the term 'heretic' by 'separated brethren', the new status of the non-Latin mass and the goal of a 'world more Christian than not.'

The Roman Church's 'pronouncements in many other areas', facilitating the new grand strategy of ecumenical unity, represent a major departure from the historic rigidities of the faith. This unprecedented flexibility in matters of faith and practice signals the determination of the Vatican to follow through on the strategy.

For example, recruitment to the 'Priesthood' has been a problem in recent years. One reason certainly is that in a world of so many diversions and so much temptation, those who sincerely opt for celibacy are far less in evidence. Certainly there are increasing numbers of priests leaving the ministry in order to get married. In recognition of this the Vatican has set in motion what has been termed 'a quiet revolution'. Married priests, mainly former Anglicans, have been ordained and permitted to take Mass, both in the UK and the USA, with the approval of the Pope. 'Pastoral provision' has been established by which they could enter the Church, and the validity of Anglican Orders has not proved to be an obstacle. There are now married parish priests and curates working in parishes.

Here we see the actual outworking of the policy of facing both ways at the same time. The official line is that the Pope still holds rigorously to a rule of celibacy for his ministers, and married priests will only be used in 'unique situations' and as 'individual concessions', which have 'no relevance to the broader debate within the Catholic Church.'

Another answer to what is a recognised problem of dwindling numbers may have been found for the closing years of the millenium in the *Decade of Evangelization* and a new *Post-Synodal Apostolic Exhortation* of the Pope. 'Dearth of priests means birth of laity' and 'Green light for laity' were two of the leader items in the *Catholic Herald* of 3rd February 1989. The Editorial describes the Pope's Apostolic Exhortation, released that week, *Christifideles Laici* (The lay members of Christ's faithful), as 'uniting as never before the efforts of clergy and laity in sanctifying the world.' Evangelization 2000 which focuses the enthusiasm and drive of large numbers of committed Catholic laity undoubtably will help to resolve the problem.

The Ordination of Women

Without question, the decision in November, 1992, of the Church of England's Synod to ordain women priests appears to present an insuperable obstacle to Anglican unity with Rome. Yet with the rapidly changing attitudes in the world, this issue, already dividing Catholics, could well become subject to the new ecumenical flexibility that has evolved out of Vatican II. How well entrenched in Church dogma will it prove to be? The recent tolerance displayed towards celibacy and married priests perhaps points the way to a major change in the not too distant future.[1] In fact there are precedents for women priests within the Roman Catholic tradition. In pre-Reformation times, both St Bridget of Kildaire and Theodora of Smyrna were priests, and both actually performed the role of a bishop.

Cardinal O'Fiaich, the late Primate of all Ireland, observed in January 1989, that 'he would not be surprised if at some future stage the Roman Church had women priests. ... I must admit that if Rome decided in the morning that women were to be admitted to the priesthood, it wouldn't cause me the slightest difficulty.' (*Catholic Herald*, 3rd February 1989). Certainly the Roman Catholic Church has need of more priests.

However many Anglican traditionalists, having lost their battle against women priests within the Church of England, under the banner 'Cost of Conscience', are organising themselves to continue the struggle elsewhere. Large numbers of them, led by former Bishop of London, Graham Leonard, are looking, in his words, to 'approach Rome as suppliants and without presumption, asking if a way could be found somehow to preserve our Anglican identity while being in Communion with the See of St Peter'. Bishop Leonard has suggested a Papal 'Personal Prelature', a special privilege granted so far only to Opus Dei.

As the traditionalists depart Romeward, the victorious liberals in the Church of England are likely to press ahead with other 'progressive' legislation favouring, or at least tolerating, abortion, homosexuality and probably adultery. Meanwhile the Church of Rome joined by Anglicans who refuse to compromise, is seen to tighten up its moral stance with the new Catechism issued in 1992. The Church of

---

[1] In the United States, a major policy statement, prepared for Catholic bishops, affirming Roman Catholic policy on women's's issues was given only 55.5% support, well short of the two-thirds needed for approval. The upshot is that the US bishops have made women's ordination subject to continuing debate. (*Time* magazine: 30th November, 1992)

England continues to disintegrate as Rome looks to the world ever more like the real church in this land.

Papal Primacy

The other theological issue which seems to be a road-block to the 're-unification' of the British Church is Papal primacy. Before Archbishop of Canterbury, Robert Runcie, visited the Pope in Rome in September 1989, he was quoted as saying: 'Anglicans are beginning to recognise and receive with favour a model of papal supremacy as a blueprint for unity with Roman Catholics.' Dr Runcie's statement and the visit was greeted by a sceptical and in part hostile press reaction. However, significantly, it opened up a national debate about Church, Crown and Constitution in a way never experienced before. The once unmentionable is now open to public discussion; the sacrosanct is no longer sacred. We have now the beginning of a process of re-education, dealing with the differences and difficulties of reconciling Lambeth and Rome, Protestant and Roman Catholic, Papal Primacy and the Monarchy. Impossibility soon becomes difficulty and the irreconcilable is reconciled. The radical shift in public opinion over close-to-home moral issues, such as homosexuality, adultery and abortion, all forbidden in the Bible, illustrates the soft backbone of public opinion.

A monarch particularly sympathetic towards Roman Catholicism and an expedient government committed to European federalism would no doubt overcome the remaining difficulties. According to the front page leader in the *Sunday Times* of 21st January, 1990, that newspaper's poll, conducted a bare three months after all of the attention given to concerns about Papal primacy, showed that nearly half the people in Britain think that the law should be changed to allow the King or Queen to be Roman Catholic. Another front page leader in the *Sunday Telegraph* of 14th April 1991 revealed that the Princess of Wales' great great great uncle Ignatius may become a 'Saint'. Such powerful publicity linking the future Queen with the Papacy may have weakened resistance to a Catholic King or Queen.

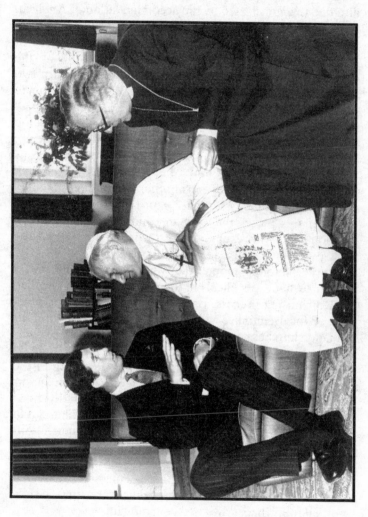

The Prince of Wales, Pope John Paul II, and Dr Robert Runcie.
© The Press Association, May 1982

Vatican Flexibility and 'the Romanising Process'

The new post-Vatican II flexibility of practice within the Roman Church that we have looked at in this chapter has also been demonstrated by the accommodation of Anglican rites, including Holy Communion, for defecting American Episcopalians. Encouraged by Rome's accommodating attitude, disillusioned Anglicans, shocked and hurt by the decision of the Church of England Synod to overturn two thousand years of tradition with the introduction of women priests and bishops, are defecting to Roman Catholicism all over the world. Such defections are certainly not hindered by the attitude of some of the Church's liberal leaders. Richard Harries, Bishop of Oxford, described a local priest's move to the Roman Catholic Church as 'not a "defection" but an opportunity to serve in another part of God's family.' (*Church of England Newspaper*, April 1989)

All of this places the Roman Church in a very strong position, and with ecumenism growing so strongly at the local level, she is well placed 'to hurry slowly'.

The accelerating momentum of the ecumenical movement, or what evangelicals in the nineteenth century called the Romanising process, is reflected in the changing practices of local churches. The great majority of Church of England churches centre their worship around the Eucharist, sometimes still called Holy Communion, rather than on the exposition of the Word of God. The reserving of the sacrament is widespread in the Church of England, and its adoration is becoming increasingly common among evangelical churches. For example the village church in Chalfont St Peter, Buckinghamshire, not thought of in the neighbourhood as being 'High Church', has a notice on the church door which reads; 'When you come into this church, remember the Lord Jesus Christ is here: he is present and to be adored under the form of the blessed Sacrament reserved for Holy Communion. Kneel down and worship Him.'

Pulpits are physically disappearing, stone and other altars reappearing, crucifixes abound, roods are returning, as are confessions and 'holy places'; and more and more ministers are styled as 'priest' and 'Father'.

'And call no man your father upon the earth: for one is your Father, which is in heaven.' Matthew 23:9

Mariolatry is no longer just the preserve of the 'High Church'. Growing devotion to Our Lady in 'Protestant' Churches is an important feature of the Ecumenical Movement. No fewer than 180 Anglican Churches have shrines to 'Our Lady of Walsingham'. Cathedrals such as at Carlisle, Chester and Chichester celebrate that which can be readily interpreted as the sacrifice of the Mass under the auspices of the new Anglican Liturgies. Interchurch and Interfaith pilgrimages are organised in increasing numbers, as devotees search for their pre-Reformation roots. The New Age Movement is not left out, and Glastonbury, centre of occult and pagan activity attracts possibly the largest numbers of pilgrims. The 1988 ecumenical celebration mass for the millenium of the death of Anglican Saint Dunstan in Glastonbury attracted a gathering of some 14,000 pilgrims, led by the Archbishop of Canterbury.

As we have seen, the media today has a crucial role in furthering 'the Romanising process' of the ecumenical movement. High profile ecumenical leaders appear regularly in the newspapers and on television. For example, Cardinal Worlock was prominent on the September 1988 BBC programme 'Songs of Praise' which explored the ecumenical dimension of the Walsingham Pilgrimage. He it was who presided over the sacrifice of the mass at Liverpool Cathedral, which was specially networked to a shaken nation after the Hillsborough football disaster in 1989. Worlock and Anglican Bishop David Sheppard, often referred to affectionately in the press as 'Tweedledum and Tweedledee' have probably between them achieved more for the ecumenical cause than anyone else in the country. Bishop Sheppard, a former England cricket captain, and Archbishop Worlock blaze the trail for ecumenical covenants and are joint authors of a book *Better Together*.

Bishop Sheppard's great predecessor at the See of Liverpool, J.C. Ryle, who foresaw the success of the Romanising process in this century, did not think that it is better together. He believed that his Bishop's allegiance to the Church of England's Articles of Faith was not negotiable.

The Rt Rev. David Sheppard, the Anglican Bishop of Liverpool, and the Most Rev. Derek Worlock, the Roman Catholic Archbishop.
© The Press Association, January 1988

Chapter 18

Peace and Evangelization 2000

The theme of peace comes up with frequent consistency. A growing world-wide consensus sees that Pope John Paul II has emerged as the great peace-maker of our day, and people are looking with renewed hope toward Rome for peace through unity. This is the man who can bring the once conflicting religions and ideologies of the world together, and more and more Christians are being convinced that he will do so under the banner of Christ.

It seems likely they will be disappointed. It is Mary, the 'Mother of God', who has spoken to the Pope about peace. Through her many appearances at Fatima, Medjugorje and elsewhere she, the 'Queen of Peace' is continually promising peace through prayer and fasting and the faithful practice of the Rosary and the pursuit of the Sacraments.

The Bible warns again and again of the false peace that the antichrist will bring:

> *'Because, even because they have seduced my people, saying, Peace; and there was no peace.'*   Ezekiel 13:10

> *'Suppose ye that I am come to give peace on earth? I tell you, Nay; but rather division.'*   Luke 12:51

We are instructed to pray for the peace of Jerusalem. The peace that the Lord has promised will come only when He comes.

Under the direction of Lutheran minister and Charismatic leader, Harald Bredesen, friend and spiritual mentor of CBN's Pat Robertson, plans were made and publicly proclaimed for Pope John Paul II to be presented with the *Prince of Peace Prize* before all the world's leaders in Washington, in 1990, to lead into the *Decade of Evangelization*. However finally it didn't happen. It may simply have been a testing of reaction to something highly controversial: if so it is only a matter of time before it actually does take place. The reaction was sadly very muted. The only previous awarding of this prize, in 1980, was to Anwar Sadat of Egypt who was assassinated very soon afterwards.

'Prince of Peace' is proposed as yet another title given to 'The Holy Father'. In the Scriptures this title belongs **only** to our Lord Jesus Christ and its usurping is profoundly shocking to Christians who regard the use by any man, of either title, as blasphemous. It is also instructive to recall that Ethiopian Emperor Haile Selasie did not live long after he proclaimed himself 'Lion of Judah'.

A definition of blasphemy has been given by the Protestant Truth Society; 'Blasphemy in Scripture means not so much speaking against God, as the assumption of Divine attributes or Divine power where no rightful claim exists.'

Much respected Roman Catholics such as Mother Teresa of Calcutta and Polish President Lech Walesa are being used by the Vatican to promote the peace theme, and behind it the plan to evangelise the earth. Both, like the Dalai Lama, have been awarded the Nobel Prize for Peace.

The 'Decade' and Growing Global Momentum

Momentum for 'the Decade' is building up as part of the Inter-Church Process with the merger of the Roman Catholic and Anglican initiatives. This merger, which inevitably offers what United Protestant Council Secretary, Anglican John Shearer, has described as 'no Gospel at all', has the blessing of the leadership of the main denominations. A letter to the *Eastern Daily Press*, in Suffolk, illustrated how the merger of the 'Protestant' and Catholic initiatives' is taking place. The letter, signed by the Anglican Bishop of Norwich and the Roman Catholic Bishop of East Anglia, called for prayer for the 'ten year programme of deepening, widening and sharing our faith, known as *The Decade of Evangelism* **or** *The Decade of Evangelization*.'

10 yrs or "Decade" of "Evang".

188

The 'Decade of Evangelization', known as *Evangelization 2000*, was launched in Britain, alongside the Decade of Evangelism and on the same day, 6th January 1991. Officially blessed at John Paul II's private Mass on 23rd June 1987, 'Evangelization 2000' reaches its climax on Christmas Day in the year 2000, when the Pope hopes to speak to five billion people in one world-wide satellite broadcast.

Fr Tom Forrest has declared that the objective of the Decade of Evangelization is to give Jesus Christ a 2000th birthday present of a world more Christian than not. The Church of England and Free Church denominations have not been so unbiblically specific about prospective conversions but have declared the aim to fulfil the Great Commission *'to preach the Gospel to all the world.'* (Mark 16:15)

The campaign is highly structured with key Vatican departments involved and most countries have a National Service Committee reporting in to the Vatican. Tom Forrest heads the office in Rome alongside fellow American Ken Metz, head of the international Catholic Charismatic Renewal office; but as Forrest said in 1989, pointing to the weighty backing of the project; 'everything is now receiving guidance from Secretary of State, Cardinal Agostino Casaroli, and from the Vatican Secretariat of Christian Unity.'

Gatherings like Acts '86, the 1987 Congress in New Orleans, 1988 in Chicago, Berlin, and 'Washington for Jesus', 1990 in Indianapolis and in Berne, through other Charismatic leaders like John Wimber, Bob Mumford, Larry Christenson, Vinson Synan and Michael Harper have given the Vatican the same message, that they are united with Roman Catholics in the plan to evangelize the world. They have also given considerable impetus to the launch of 'Evangelization 2000' among Pentecostals and Charismatics.

Brighton 91, 'That the world may believe', which took place in July 1991, was described by its organisers who included Chairman Michael Harper, Dr Vinson Synan, Larry Christenson, Fr Tom Forrest and fellow Roman Catholic Mrs Kim Kollins, as being able to 'provide the greatest potential today for achieving the target of reaching the world through this coming decade.'

Pastor Ron Smith of the Kent-based Fishers Fellowship expressed the deep concern of many evangelicals that the euphoria of it all would break down any barriers or reservations some might have. 'I believe, he wrote in January 1991, 'that at Brighton there will be unity of heart and emotions. The worship group will ensure this. There will be sincere fervour as delegates sing "Jesus is Lord". Some will hold hands, sway, fall down or dance. There will be genuine tears of joy as some fellowship with those with whom they have never done so before. It will not however constitute a unity in the gospel. It will be the kind of emotional unity that is expressed at the last night of the "Prom's" as thousands sing "Land of Hope and Glory".'

Large numbers of the world's Evangelical leaders attended *Lausanne 1989*, the second international congress on world evangelisation. The conference, which took place in Manila in July 1989, according to its programme, 'sought to coordinate a plethora of strategies which have been formulated to evangelise the world by the year 2000 AD.' The first *Lausanne Congress* in 1974 invited five WCC leaders and three Roman Catholic priests as observers. (*FEA News and Views*, July/August 1974).

Although the Roman Catholic Church is not one of the 317 member churches of the World Council of Churches, Roman Catholics play a major role in the work of the Council. The WCC staff are drawn from 89 different member churches, but about 25% belong to just one church, the Roman Catholic Church. Moreover, the Vatican appoints 12 of the 120 members of the WCC Commission on Faith and Order and sent 23 observers to the recent *Seventh Assembly* in Canberra, Australia, in February 1991. This Assembly, with its theme 'Come Holy Spirit – Renew the Whole Creation', broke new ground in the promotion of other faiths and one world religion.

Following the Leader

Well known leading Protestants including Jim Packer and Chuck Colson write in Christian Publications such as the magazine *New Covenant*, the pre-eminent periodical of the

Catholic Renewal. These magazines simultaneously promote aspects of the Catholic faith including the Rosary, visitations at Medjugorje and prayers to Mary and the saints, whilst publicising 'Evangelization 2000' and 'The Decade of Evangelization', gathering momentum for this global evangelistic undertaking.

John Wimber, a greatly respected and very influential leader among Charismatic Christians, has been used in this way. An article by him in the June 1988 edition of New Covenant on 'Why I love Mary', arguing that 'Her faith is a model for our faith' appeared opposite another article, also on 'Why I love Mary', in which Mary is portrayed as the Mother who answers the prayers of the faithful.

As an enthusiastic supporter of ecumenism, John Wimber, who puts special emphasis on signs and wonders in his ministry, has come out strongly in favour of Roman Catholic evangelism; 'Since Pope John XXIII called Vatican II and prayed 'Come Holy Spirit, we need a new Pentecost,' there has been an explosion in the Church,' he said. (John Wimber: *MC510 Manual*, Fuller Seminary, California)

John Wimber strongly endorsed the ministries of a group of Old Testament-style prophets, centred at Kansas City, the first major ecumenical conference venue of the Renewal. These 'Kansas City prophets', were said to have successfully predicted earthquake and drought. They prophesied revival falsely, and with prophesies not limited to Scripture, were the cause of major divisions within the Charismatic Church. Before their leader, Paul Cain, left to join in ministry with Westminster Chapel pastor, R.T. Kendall, they were endorsed at their 1990 introduction in London by Terry Virgo, Roger Forster, Gerald Coates, Lynn Green, Sandy Millar, David Pytches and other Charismatic leaders.

The prophets do not have the endorsement of Scripture;

'God, who at sundry times and in divers manners spoke in time past unto the fathers by the prophets, hath in these last days spoken unto us by His Son, whom He hath appointed heir of all things.' Hebrews 1:1 & 2

Vision: A.D. 2000

Remarkable numbers of local churches and fellowships have a vision for growth into the 21st century and are gearing up to participate in ecumenical evangelism in the years ahead. Modern marketing methods are now 'in', and much is communicated to congregations about 'strategy', 'planning for growth' and 'vision' with numbers targeted for the 1990s. Evangelical organisations are proliferating new 'brands' and 'trademarks' such as Target 2000, Faith 2000, Vision 21st Century, Countdown 2000, Lumen 2000, Mission 2000, Reaching the World 2000 and AD 2000 World Evangelization Movement.

The year 2000 is also of great significance to New Agers. According to New Age thinking, the Vernal Equinox pointing now to Pisces (fish), the Age of the Church, will move by the year 2000 to the Age of Aquarius (the water-bearer) and the end of strife on earth. The Age of Aquarius is another name for the New Age , seen by some observers as yet another elaborate Counter-Reformation smokescreen to cause God's people to drop their guard, to succumb to 'futurist' thinking and look to the future for the antichrist.

Chapter 19

Bible Prophecy and Bible Versions

The author recognizes that for all the weight of evidence, all the lessons of history, all the testimony of great men, the reader will not fully recognize the role of Rome, nor the roads which lead to her, unless God, in His grace, quickens the understanding through His Word. An understanding of the interpretation of Bible prophecy held by the reformers and those who have stood up to Rome before and since, is therefore important to the message of this book.

Many Protestant commentators point out that the interpretation of Biblical prophecy is now almost all 'Futurist', the system which they believe was evolved by the brilliant Jesuit theologians Ribera and Bellarmine after the *Council of Trent*. They see futurist scholars as evolving eschatological theories and systems faster than theological colleges can absorb them. The view that the antichrist is still to come, and that therefore the passages of Scripture relating to him are not for today, has undermined the faith of Bible-believing Christians, they believe, and is the principal reason why so few now recognize the office of the Papacy in Scripture as the false church which has opposed the true faith for almost 1500 years.

Other Protestants do not agree that the emphasis on a future antichrist subtracts from the witness of Christians to the errors of Rome. 'Thousands, nay, tens of thousands of Bible believers who believe in a future person, *the* antichrist, are utterly opposed to Rome', says Bicester-based businessman, Michael Penfold. 'Jesuits have not undermined their faith since the Bible declares that there were *many* anti-christs in the days of the apostles.'

There is no question, however, that Futurism and Praeter-ism have made a profound impact on Bible colleges and pulpits alike during this century and most of the last century. These theories were propounded by the Jesuits as powerful instruments of the Counter-Reformation, soon after the Council of Trent, but made little impact until the nineteenth century. The Roman Catholic 'Truth Society' has defined the two schools of interpretation of Scripture as follows:

> 'The Praeterist school founded by the Jesuit Alcazar in 1614 explains the book of Revelation by the fall of Jerusalem in AD 70, or by the fall of pagan Rome in AD 410 ... The Futurist school founded by the Jesuit Ribera in 1591 looks for antichrist, Babylon and a rebuilt temple in Jerusalem, at the end of the Christian Dispensation.'

Jesuit Futurism and Praeterism, in opposition to what was the prevailing view of Christians, now known as the 'Histor-icist' or historical view, set out originally to divorce the antichrist, the man of sin, the little horn and the Mother of Harlots from the here and now, and from mediaeval and modern history. Between them these interpretations suc-ceeded in excluding the entire fifteen century period of the Papacy altogether from the understanding of Bible proph-ecy. They did so by stopping short of the beginnings of the Roman Church in the fifth century and then by projecting forward beyond our day into a fragment of time in the indeterminate future.

The 'Historicist', or historical view sees the prophecies of Daniel, Paul and John as fully and faithfully laying out the entire course of Christian history. It recognizes the Roman Institution which claims to be the Universal Church as the whore posing as the Bride of Christ, and identifies *the little horn* of *Daniel 7*, *the man of sin* of *2 Thessalonians 2* and the *Mother of Harlots* of *Revelation 17 & 18* as the Papacy and the false Church.

194

'There are two great truths that stand out in the preaching that brought about the Protestant Reformation,' American Bible commentator, Ralph Woodrow, reminds us; 'The just shall live by faith, not by the works of Romanism and the Papacy is the antichrist of Scripture. It was a message for Christ and against antichrist. The entire Reformation rests on this twofold testimony.' Iain Murray, in his much respected book *The Puritan Hope* describes the Reformers as 'unanimous in their belief that the Papal system is both *the man of sin* and the Babylonian whore of which Scripture forewarns. Rome was the great antichrist, and so firmly did this belief become established that it was not until the nineteenth century that it was seriously questioned by evangelicals.' (Iain Murray: *The Puritan Hope*, Banner of Truth)

'Thousands of martyrdoms have sealed the testimony against the Papal antichrist, said Grattan Guinness at the end of the nineteenth century, 'and on this testimony rests the Reformation. To reject it is to reject the foundation of the noblest and divinest work which has been wrought in this world since the day of Pentecost.' (Dr H. Grattan Guinness DD, FRAS – *Romanism and the Reformation*: Focus Christian Ministries: Orchard Road, Lewes, East Sussex.)

The Little Horn of Daniel

The Reformers identified the Papacy in the persecuting little horn of the Book of Daniel. John Wycliffe asked, 'why is it necessary in unbelief to look for another antichrist? In the seventh chapter of of Daniel, antichrist is forcefully described by a horn arising in the time of the fourth kingdom wearing out the saints of the most high.' (Leroy Froom – *The Prophetic Faith of Our Fathers*)

The Reformers believed, as do many Christians today, that the little horn of Daniel 7 had risen out of the fourth beast, the Roman Empire, and sprung up among the ten kingdoms into which Imperial Rome was divided. The little horn is *diverse* or different from the other kingdoms; the Papacy claimed spiritual as well as temporal power. The little horn has *a mouth that spake very great things* and *shall speak great words against the most High*. Over the centuries the Papacy has repeatedly laid claim to rule the world as Christ's representative and insisted that there is no salvation outside of the Church of Rome. (Boniface VIII: *Unam Sanctam*) It has also claimed to speak with infallibility on matters of faith and doctrine, usurping God's authority and contradicting His Word.

In Daniel's vision, the little horn *had eyes* and *his look was more stout than his fellows*. The Pope, who lays claim to the keys to the kingdom of heaven, is said to watch over more people than any other leader. He is responsible for pastoring some 900 million souls across the world today.

The little horn *made war with the saints and prevailed against them ... and would wear out the saints of the most High*. Many believe that this part of the prophecy was comprehensively fulfilled over the many centuries of Papal Rome's ruthless persecution of Bible-believing Christians; through the Dark Ages, during the Inquisition and right up to the French Revolution.

The little horn would *think to change times and laws*. The Papacy has not only changed human laws but divine laws too. It has annulled and abrogated the laws of kings and emperors and relatively recently, in 1870, claimed itself infallible in defiance of Scripture. It has presumed to annul marriages and ordain a celibate 'Priesthood' in place of the Biblical model of married pastors. Times have been changed too. The calendar of Pope Gregory has replaced the calendar of the Emperor Justinian. There are all the many different 'Saints' days, and we have 'Christ's Mass' or Christmas to celebrate Our Lord's birth and the pagan Goddess Astarte's festival, Easter, for His death and resurrection.

The Man of Sin and the Mystery of Iniquity

The 'Pontifical', the special Service book used for Papal services in St Peter's, Rome, addresses the reigning Pontiff with the dreadful words, 'Lord God the Pope'. Writing to the Christians in Thessalonika, Paul describes the 'Man of Sin', the 'Son of Perdition':

196

*... and that man of sin be revealed, the son of perdition;
Who opposeth and exalteth himself above all that is
called God, or that is worshipped; so that he as God
sitteth in the temple of God, showing himself that he is
God.*   2 Thessalonians 2:3 & 4

There seems to have been a remarkable consensus of
understanding among the early church fathers and the
Reformers in equating the little horn with the man of sin
revealed by Paul in the second letter to the Thessalonians.
They believed that *the man of sin* and *the mystery of iniquity
already at work* in Paul's day would follow the fall of the
Roman Empire.

*For the mystery of iniquity doth already work; only he
who now letteth will let, until he be taken out of the way.
And then shall that Wicked be revealed ...*
                                        verses 7 & 8

The Encyclopaedia Britannica records that during those
first centuries, 'Christians universally believed that the
power that was retarding the revelation of the antichrist
was the Roman Empire.' It was and still is widely understood that the Apostle wrote to the Thessalonians myster-
iously about the restraining of the antichrist, that 'he (not
He, as in some Bible versions) who letteth will now let,
until he be taken out of the way,' because he was referring
to Imperial Rome. Had he been more explicit and spelled
out his belief that Imperial Rome, which was restraining
the antichrist, would fall at some undetermined time, he
would have brought the Christians, especially those in Thessalonika into conflict with the ruling power.

Witnesses to the Truth

Wycliffe, Tyndale, Luther, Calvin, Cranmer; in the seven-
teenth century, Bunyan, the translators of the King James
Bible and the men who published the Westminster and
Baptist Confessions of Faith; Sir Isaac Newton, Wesley,
Whitfield, Jonathan Edwards; and more recently,

Spurgeon, Bishop J.C. Ryle and Dr Martyn Lloyd-Jones; these men among countless others, all saw the office of the Papacy as the antichrist, that is substituting for Christ, the new face of the old paganism that is *Mystery Babylon* in the Bible. They saw it all in the Scriptures, it was quickened to them. They saw the counterfeit Bride, the Whore which would be judged at the end of history, in the description of Revelation 17, as do so many others today;

> *I will show unto thee the judgment of the great whore that sitteth upon many waters. With whom the kings of the earth have committed fornication, and the inhabitants of the earth have been made drunk with the wine of her fornication. So he carried me away in the spirit into the wilderness: and I saw a woman sit upon a scarlet coloured beast, full of names of blasphemy, having seven heads and ten horns. And the woman was arrayed in purple and scarlet colour, and decked with gold and precious stones and pearls, having a golden cup in her hand full of abominations and filthiness of her fornication: And upon her forehead was a name written, MYSTERY, BABYLON THE GREAT, THE MOTHER OF HARLOTS AND ABOMINATIONS OF THE EARTH. And I saw the woman drunken with the blood of the saints, and with the blood of the martyrs of Jesus: and when I saw her, I wondered with great admiration.*

The Reformers saw the system for what it was and they knew that they had to stand clearly against it. If they were right about that then, they are still right about it now. God's Word does not change.

These were the men described by one of their number, John Knox, as 'they that love the coming of the Lord.' All were immensely burdened for the souls of those in bondage to such an evil and corrupt system, imprisoned in what Martin Luther called *the Babylonian Captivity of the Church.*

The Reformers and their heirs were great scholars and knew the Word of God and the Holy Spirit as a living teacher. They recognized and identified the false interpretations of Bible prophecy and the scholarly deceptions of the Jesuits and the Counter-Reformation and they *'earnestly contended for the faith once given to the saints'*. (Jude 3) They knew that it is the responsibility of all Christians to be a watchman, not just a special few with a special 'prophetic calling' to speak out. From soon after the Reformation until late in the nineteenth century their Historical interpretation of the antichrist in Scripture was to be found in the majority of Bible commentaries. This is no longer true today. In fact we know of no Bible commentary, published in the last fifty years, that adopts this position.

Bible Versions: Protestantism and Ecumenism

The principal reason for this is the proliferation of the new 'modern' versions, and commentaries, mostly based on the scholarship of the 1881 Revising Committee led by Anglo-Catholic Cambridge Professors Westcott and Hort. Adherents of the King James or Authorised version are convinced that the texts adopted by the revised and modern versions are those which, as long ago as the fourth century, were rejected as corrupted during a period of Arian influence, and which were subsequently discarded by the Reformation.

The view of leading Protestant scholars today is that the King James Version is the only truly Protestant Bible, and the only one which really lends itself to the historical interpretation of the antichrist.[1] Virtually all the other translations are regarded as having leanings towards Liberalism and Romanism, clearly favouring the futurist view in the prophetic passages discussed earlier in this chapter. Even

---

[1] The author has written a booklet on Bible versions and the interpretation of Bible prophecy, *All's Well or Sound the Alarm*, which affirms the reliability and purity of the Authorised Version (KJV) and argues that the Scriptures have been undermined, and the Gospel watered down by the existence of a seemingly unending range of 'Bibles'. It seems that the 'Thus saith the Lord' of the old Authorised has given place among the many modern versions, and the choice of rendering of any particular verse that they afford, to 'has God said?' (Genesis 3:1)

All's Well or Sound the Alarm: Spirit of '88, 1989 – see list at end of book.

the New King James version which, like the KJV, uses the Textus Receptus, rather than the Minority texts Vaticanus and Sinaiticus favoured by the new editions, adopts this same futurist rendering, postponing the fulfilment of anti-christ into the indefinite future.

Ecumenism and the NIV

The Ecumenical Movement has ensured continuing cooperation among Catholics and 'Protestants' on Bible translations, and there have been innumerable conferences. The Driebergen Conference, held in June, 1964, and attended by representatives of the United Bible Societies and the Roman Catholic Church, proposed the preparation of a 'common text' of the Bible, and a 'common translation', which would be acceptable to all. In 1965, the Second Vatican Council ratified the Roman Church's approval of this, and, in 1967, Carlo Martini joined the UBS International Editorial Committee.

Carlo Martini is His Eminence Cardinal Carlo Maria Martini, Archbishop of Milan, the Vatican's predominant Greek scholar, a Jesuit, who is thought of as a likely successor to Pope John Paul. He is President of the Council of European Bishop's Conferences, which represents 133,000 European churches. Cardinal Martini was a member of the UBS editorial committee for both the second and third editions of the Greek New Testament.

The Third Edition of the United Bible Societies' Greek New Testament, published in 1975, is a complete revision of the text produced previously, incorporating more than five hundred changes which were made by Cardinal Carlo Martini and his four colleagues. The Third Edition was first issued several years before it was actually published. Its preface states that *A Textual Commentary on the Greek New Testament* (1971), edited by Bruce M. Metzger on behalf of the Committee, is based on this Third Edition.' The Second Edition was produced three years earlier in 1968, so 'it appears that with no significant accretion of new evidence, the same group of five scholars changed their mind in over five hundred places. It is hard to resist the suspicion that they are guessing.' (Wilbur N. Pickering: *The Identity of the New Testament Text*: Thomas Nelson, Nashville, 1980)

The new Latin Vulgate, authorised by Pope Paul VI in 1965, was issued by the Vatican and published by the German Bible Society (a member of UBS), in 1979, with a corrected Latin text which 'conforms' to the same UBS Third Edition of the Greek New Testament.

In that same year, 1979, the German Bible Society published the twenty-sixth edition of the *Nestle-Aland Greek New Testament* with a Greek text absolutely identical to the UBS Third Edition.

The New Testament of the *New International Version* is based on the UBS/Nestle-Aland Greek New Testament, as are the majority of modern translations, including *The New Revised Standard Version, The New American Standard Version, The Revised English Bible* and *The Good News Bible*. According to the International Bible Society, quoting Kenneth L. Barker's book, *The NIV: The Making of a Contemporary Translation*, the cryptic 'eclectic' Greek New Testament text used was 'basically that found in the United Bible Societies' and Nestle's printed Greek New Testaments, which contain the latest and best Greek text available.'

Some Christians have suggested that the NIV could be called the 'New Catholic Version', given that the word 'catholic' means 'universal' or 'international', and many evangelicals see the wide distribution of these 'Ecumenical' Bibles, based on a 'common text' authorised by the Vatican, as an essential step towards union with Rome.

Chapter 20

'Another Gospel': Conversion to Christ

We are living in a challenging time for Christians, a time of massive indifference to the Gospel across society. Liberal Christianity which denies the great truths of the faith; higher criticism and the new hermeneutic among theologians; the rapid rise of Islam and other world religions; the growth of the Mormons, the Jehovah Witnesses and the other cults; as well as the advance of Multi-Faith religion and the formidable New Age movement; all these are absorbing the spiritual firepower of God's people.

There are so many battles to fight and so many enemies to face, that, understandably, followers of Christ are eager to join with those who have firm beliefs on the Virgin Birth and the Resurrection; and who also hold to clear Biblical positions on the great issues of social concern.

The charismatic movement, with its healings and other signs and wonders, with its impressive unity among denominations and apparent warmth and joy among so many of those involved, seems to be empowered to *fight the good fight*. But the parables of Matthew 13, those of the sower and the wheat and the tares, remind us that the church just isn't like this. All is not as it seems. The majority who 'make commitments' with joy grow no roots, succumb to the comforts and lures of the world and fall away usually only when the going gets difficult. They may continue to feature strongly in the church; praise, pray and prophesy but they seek to serve both the world and God.

*Narrow is the way which leads to life and few there be
that find it.'*   Matthew 7:14

The pastoral implications of all this for individuals and
for the churches are clearly sensitive and invidious. The
challenge in the closing years of this century and millennium for Protestants is to reassert Biblical truths and to
proclaim the need for a New Reformation. Holy Spirit
revival is the earnest prayer of every God-fearing church.
The need for repentance before God and for the forthright
opposing of false doctrine with Scriptural truth, is generally
acknowledged.

Martyn Lloyd-Jones, who was greatly burdened for those
trapped within the sacramental and sacerdotal system, felt
that only when sound Biblical doctrine came together with
experience of the power and gifts given by the Spirit could
the balance be right. He was deeply troubled by a dry,
intellectual, critical, and fearful Christianity, which
rejected all experience and the fullness of God's provision
by His Spirit. For him, both reformation and renewal were
needed for revival.

The power of God and the work of the Holy Spirit should
not be denied simply because the counterfeit is so widespread. Those who, like Dr Lloyd-Jones, believe in God's
sovereignty over the provision of spiritual gifts, are concerned that too many churches, fearful of deception, are
prone to throw out the baby with the bathwater.

The Charismatic Renewal has brought many to a knowledge of the Word of God, but all too rarely with the
reverence that is due to a God who is holy. Spiritual discernment is scarce; tolerance towards the teaching of *'those
that trouble you, and would pervert the gospel of Christ'*
(Galatians 1:7) is a feature of our times. Might such tolerance be a denial of pastoral responsibility?

Believers have to face up to the rising influence of
*'another spirit, which ye have not received, or another gospel
which ye have not accepted.'* (2 Corinthians 11:4) What is
called for is more clarity, more discernment and more
vigilance. Either to decide to please men or to please God
and choose to publicly endorse or deny Roman Catholicism. In opposing error, we must make clear the crucial

203

distinction between Roman Catholicism and Roman Catholics, the religious system and the people within it.

There simply isn't any middle ground. Catholics themselves have ever been crystal clear about that; 'The Roman Church is either the masterpiece of Satan or the kingdom of the Son of God,' insisted Cardinal Manning. His contemporary and colleague, Cardinal Newman was just as emphatic; 'A sacerdotal order (of priesthood) is historically the essence of the Church of Rome; if not divinely appointed, it is doctrinally the essence of antichrist.' (*Romanism and the Reformation* : Dr H. Grattan Guinness: Focus, 1987)

To vacillate in today's climate, with such a strong ecumenical current flowing, is to appear to endorse Rome's errors. Not to speak out is to deny the truth to all those in the Anglican and Catholic churches still entangled in the man-made bondage of ritualism, and depending on the sacraments and the Priesthood for the grace of God. In appearing alongside prominent Roman Catholics at conferences and in ecumenical enterprises, even merely as a name on the notepaper, evangelical leaders are effectively endorsing unscriptural beliefs. The New Testament is as clear as the Old about separation;

> *'And have no fellowship with the unfruitful works of darkness, but rather reprove them.'*   Ephesians 5:11

> *'Wherefore come out from among them, and be ye separate, saith the Lord, and touch not the unclean thing; and I will receive you.'*   2 Corinthians 6:17

Dr Francis Schaeffer thought that in facing up to this issue, 'three choices exist. Unloving confrontation, no confrontation and loving confrontation. Only the third is biblical.' Those leaders in the churches who understand the problem and its dangers, and who excuse themselves saying, 'this is not my particular calling' or 'the timing is not right', are not in accord with the scriptures. As the much respected Bible Commentator, Matthew Henry, said: 'Evil abounds when good men stay silent.'

Attitudes to Individual Roman Catholics

To confront the error is not to condemn the person. Leading Protestant protagonist and 'watchman', Albert Close, writing in the 194Os, represented the view of evangelical Christianity when he declared;

> 'The author believes and unhesitatingly acknowledges that many Roman Catholics are real children of God. They have believed on Christ in spite of all the mystic Pagan rites, ceremonies and doctrines under which the priesthood has buried the Truth. They are better than their creed. Millions of them are in heaven today. Some, like Bernard of Clairvaux, have been God's choicest spirits. But the Papal religious system which has "imprisoned the Truth in unrighteousness" is the Devil's travesty of Divine Truth. God does care whether man worships in a right, or in a wrong and forbidden way. God's fiercest anger with old Israel was aroused because Israel would persist in worshipping in a wrong and forbidden way, setting up images and bowing down before them.' (*The Divine Programme of the World's History by A. Close*)

To question the salvation of individual Catholics, especially those 'baptized in the Spirit' in the renewal is sure to be seen as bigoted and sectarian. But California's Bill Jackson of *Christians Evangelising Catholics* argues: 'To tell the truth is not bigotry or hatred. If you hated anyone who is lost, you would leave them alone and let them go to hell.'

Charismatics are right to say that truth without love is bigotry; but 'love without truth is whoredom' says Protestant publisher Jack Chick, another Californian.

'If you love me, keep my commandments,' said Jesus. (John 14:15). If you love those in error you will tell them the Truth. *'Preach the Word; be instant in and out of season; reprove, rebuke, exhort with all long-suffering and doctrine.'* (2 Timothy 4:2)

Advising individuals, tied to the sacraments for the remission of their sins, about the true nature of a faith they have pursued for much of their lives requires special sensitivity, discernment and knowledge, as well as much prayer. However those who are truly converted and who continue to participate in the Mass, and in what was until recently known as the confessional, and in prayers to the Virgin Mary and the Saints, are sure to feel uncomfortable as their understanding is quickened by Holy Scripture.

The Good News – Conversion to Christ

In the Gospel of Matthew, Jesus differentiates between religion and saving faith.

> 'Enter ye in at the strait gate: for wide is the gate, and broad is the way, that leadeth to destruction, and many there be that go in thereat: because strait is the gate, and narrow is the way, which leadeth unto life, and few there be that find it.'   Matthew 7:13, 14

Good works, the sacraments and Baptism are an expression of the life of Christ within us and our love for Christ, but they play no part in our salvation. It is impossible to please God and earn grace in any of these ways. God is holy and must judge sin.

> 'As it is written, There is none righteous, no, not one. For all have sinned, and come short of the glory of God.'   Romans 3:10 & 23

All of us are deserving of His judgement.

Being raised in a Christian home won't make us a Christian, nor will church attendance; nor indeed will baptism and confirmation or participation in Communion. What then is the answer? What makes a Christian? Luther, formidable in intellect and spiritual self-discipline, long strived and searched in vain for the 'narrow road that leads to life'. The Spirit of Jesus, the living Lord, led him to the answer in the Scriptures. *The just shall live by faith,'* wrote Paul to the Christians in Rome, and *'a man is justified by faith without the deeds of the law.'* Our salvation is simply a gift; out of the amazing grace of God we are freely forgiven. We can't earn it, *'boasting is excluded'* (Habbakuk 2:4 and Romans 1:17; 3:28 & 3:27)

The blessed assurance of personal salvation depends entirely on a wonderful historical fact – Christ died, on the cross, as the Passover lamb, a sacrifice once and for all time for our sins. He died for us, and we die with Him to sin and self: *'Ye are dead, and your life is hid with Christ in God'* (Colossians 3:3). We rise again with Him into new life by the resurrection power of the Holy Spirit. *'Therefore if any man be in Christ, he is a new creature: old things are passed away; behold' all things are become new'* (2 Corinthians 5:17).

Jesus told Nicodemus, a leader among the Sanhedrin and like the unconverted Luther well versed in theology and religion, that he needed to be *'born again ... of water and the Spirit* (John 3:3 & 5). We cannot approach God on our terms, nor through our intellects. For, *'has not God made foolish the wisdom of this world?'* (1 Corinthians 1:20). Our approach to God must be as a little child before our heavenly Father, because *'whosoever shall not receive the kingdom of God as a little child shall in no wise enter therein'* (Luke 18:17).

Londoner, Ralph Brockman, a man of prayer and member of Intercessors for Britain, recalls:

'For many years I was on that broad road, attending an Anglo-Catholic church, and I had difficulty understanding the matter of "justification by faith" and why Jesus died on the cross. I knew there was a heaven and a hell. I wanted to go to heaven, but was trying to earn my salvation. I used the following prayer:

"Oh Lord I am a sinner and I'm sorry for my sins. I'm willing to turn from my sins. I receive Jesus Christ as my Lord and Saviour. I confess Him as Lord. I want to serve Him from this moment on in the fellowship of His church. In Christ's name. Amen."'

For more information and advice concerning personal salvation, contact: Spirit of '88, Dorchester House, Marsham Lane, Gerrards Cross Bucks.

Chapter 21

Who Are These 'Protestants?'

Those who follow Christ as his disciples, sinners saved by grace, believe in the power of prayer. Scripture confirms their belief: *The effectual fervent prayer of a righteous man availeth much'*. (James 5:16) They know that they have been redeemed through the shed blood of Christ and born again of His Spirit. They believe that Christ came to die for them so that they might live entirely for Him. The wonderful assurance of Salvation is the very basis of their lives.

They find that they hate sin and love Christ. They are not 'religious' and dislike ritual. They recognise only two God-ordained sacraments, Baptism and 'The Lord's Supper', for those who have been born again into a new life in Christ. They seek to be led by one Spirit and base their convictions on one book, 'and that book the Bible'.

They believe in the God who heals and does miracles, when He in His sovereign majesty purposes to do so. They may or may not believe that all the gifts of the Spirit are for today. Compared with the great truths for which they contend, such differences in the interpretation of Scripture are of small account. They are open to other points of view, and always alive and receptive to what God might do. They are discerning and alert to deception and infiltration. *'For I know this, that after my departing shall grievous wolves enter in among you, not sparing the flock'*. (Acts 20:29)

When not actually persecuted for their beliefs, they tend to be seen as sectarian, as conservative to the extent of being negative; as well as bigoted and sometimes unloving.

John Kennedy, the Scottish Highland evangelist wrote; 'no Christian can be true and faithful on whose brow the world shall not brand the name bigot. But let him bear it. It is a mark of honour, though intended to be a brand of shame. In every age from the beginning, when the cause of truth emerged triumphant from the din and dust of controversy, the victory was won by a band of bigots who were sworn to its defence.' Let C.H. Spurgeon be their spokesman;

> 'I believe and glory in that which at present is so much spoken against, sectarianism. If a man be earnest about Truth, he will be sectarian. When we cease to strive, seek, contend and maintain the Truth, it will cease in our land and error alone shall reign.'

The Bible describes these servants of God as *saints* and as *a royal priesthood.* (1 Peter 2:9), but they never amount to much in their own eyes. Only Christ matters to them . One among the greatest of them expressed this for all, in his letter to the Philippians; *For to me to live is Christ, and to die is gain,* (i.e. more of Him) wrote the Apostle Paul (Philippians 1:21) and *'I am crucified with Christ: nevertheless I live; yet not I, but Christ lives in me.'* (Galatians 2:20)

After all, the Lord had made it clear enough; *Whosoever will come after me, let him deny himself, and take up his cross, and follow me.* (Mark 8:34) A handful of Christians without political power and without armies (and certainly without sectarian violence or retaliation) changed the world again and again. God acted and God was glorified. Their successors are among us today, a remnant, scattered and often isolated among the denominations.

'This is the church which does the work of Christ on earth,' wrote Bishop J.C. Ryle, 'Its members are a little flock, and few in number, one or two here and two or three there – a few in this district and a few in that. But these are they who shake the universe; who change the fortune of kingdoms by their prayers; these are they who are the active workers for spreading the knowledge of pure religion and undefiled; these are the lifeblood of the country, the shield, the defence, the stay, and the support of any nation to which they belong.' (*The True Church* by Dr J.C. Ryle)

Controversy in religion, as Bishop Ryle reminded the church, is a hateful thing.

> 'It is hard enough to fight the Devil, the world and the flesh without private differences in our own camp. But there is one thing that is even worse than controversy, and that is false doctrine tolerated and permitted without protest and molestation. It was controversy that won the battle of the Protestant Reformation. If the views which some men hold were correct it is plain that we ought not to have had a Reformation at all. For the sake of peace we should have gone on worshipping the Virgin, and bowing down to images and relics to this day. The Apostle Paul was the most divisive and controversial character in the entire book of Acts, and because of it he was beaten with rods, stoned and left as dead, chained and left in a dungeon, dragged before magistrates, barely escaped assassination, and so pronounced in him were his convictions that it came to a point when the unbelieving Jews in Thessalonica declared: "These that have turned the world upside down are come hither also." God pity those pastors whose main objective is the growth of their organisations and whose main concern lest their "boats be rocked." They may escape involvement in controversy, but they will not escape the judgement seat of Christ.'

Contending for the Faith

One Englishman who, not so very long ago, contended for the faith in the face of enormous controversy, was John Kensit. His protest in 1898 at St Cuthbert's Church was the most famous of many that he made over what the Archbishop of Canterbury and others of that day later referred to, at an ecclesiastical enquiry into Kensit's death, as 'grievous departures from the Reformed position of the English Church.' Kensit was assassinated in Liverpool; a sharp instrument was plunged into his eye, during a mission that he was leading with the newly formed Wycliffe Preachers in that city. Writing in 1902, just after Kensit died as a martyr for the Truth, the Revd J.C. Wilcox caught the spirit of this man of God in describing the famous protest at St Cuthbert's:

'The beacon fires of 1588 have died down. Their ashes are scattered to the four winds ... But other fires of the same century have never gone out – no, nor ever can! The Martyr-fires of the glorious Reformation are burning still. The spirit of the martyrs is still unconsumed. The candle lighted at many a stake has never been put out. Little did I know that at that very hour, (when Wilcox was reading a draft of the first edition of the *Beacon Fire*), on Good Friday 1898, in a West End Church, a man whose spirit was ablaze with the flame from the altar-fires of Truth, and in whose bones there burned the consuming fire of righteous indignation at untruth and idolatry, a man whose lips had been touched with a live coal from off the martyrs' fires of the Reformation – little did I dream that at that now notorious Church of St Cuthbert, Philbeach Gardens, Kensington, one brave soul was giving the signal for a national rekindling of the Reformation Candle.'

'That brave man was John Kensit. And what had he done? He had attended at St Cuthbert's Church, in company with Mrs Kensit and his son, a Roman service known as "The Adoration of the Cross". In that service the vicar after uncovering the veiled crucifix said, "Behold the Wood of the Cross." To this the congregation responded, "Come let us adore it." Then the clergy, and next two by two the congregation, crawled to the crucifix, which had been laid on the chancel steps, and prostrate kissed the figures thereon. Then it was that one man, whose spirit was stirred within him at this unblushing idolatry in a parish church, felt the force of a divine call. He seized the crucifix, and holding it aloft in the face of the idolaters, said clearly and solemnly and in words befitting a

Hebrew prophet, **"In the name of God I denounce this idolatry in the Church of England. – God help me."** The trumpet blast of a second Reformation in England's Church had sounded forth. From St Cuthbert's it was destined to re-echo in every parish church in the land. Thousands and thousands of sober and conscientious and loyal sons of the national Church – who had been alienated from the Church of their forefathers – rallied at the call. The forces of Protestantism – fainting and well nigh sick at heart at the encroachments of Sacerdotalism within their beloved Church – sprang round the standard of the Reformation.' (*Contending for the Faith*: Revd J.C. Wilcox, Protestant Truth Society, 184 Fleet Street, London: 1902 and 1989)

Were Ryle and Kensit and other great men of faith alive today they would scarcely recognise the popular and comfortable form of evangelical Christianity which 'celebrates' at every opportunity and merely seeks the world's approval instead of confronting it with its sin and need for the Saviour. They would be horrified by the accommodation with false religion, knowing that this must undermine and eventually destroy the very foundation of so many lives. *'If the foundations be destroyed what can the righteous do?'* (Psalm 113) They would deplore the weak and equivocal leadership which co-exists with so many false doctrines and causes so much confusion among believers while hundreds of millions of Anglicans, Orthodox and Catholics head towards a Christless eternity.

God spoke the world into existence and Christians proclaim their faith with the spoken word. *If thou shalt confess with thy mouth the Lord Jesus, and shalt believe in thy heart that God has raised him from the dead, thou shalt be saved.* (Romans 10:9) There are no private Christians; none who have not declared their faith before men. *Whosoever therefore shall be ashamed of me and of my words in this adulterous and sinful generation', said Jesus, 'of him also shall the Son of man be ashamed...* (Mark 8:38)

Those who speak up, actively oppose and take a stand

against all compromise of Biblical truth, *earnestly contend for the faith which was once delivered unto the saints.* (Jude 3) They may be a scattered people, as were the Christians in Asia to whom Peter wrote his first letter or those to whom Bishop Ryle referred. Like their courageous forbears, surrounded by so much falsehood, confusion and compromise, they are prepared to stand their ground, holding out the light of the gospel to the deceived millions 'on the broad path to destruction'.

In an address to the British Evangelical Council in 1969, one among them, and truly a prophetic voice in his generation and beyond, expressed their likely re-action very powerfully, with a message as important today as then. Citing the Scripture in 1 Corinthians 14:8, *'For if the trumpet gives an uncertain sound who shall prepare himself to the battle?'*, Dr Martyn Lloyd-Jones made clear that he believed that the enemy are not just present but rampant in the camp; 'Sound the alarm', he thundered, 'Sound the alarm'. (Dr Martyn Lloyd-Jones: *The Trumpet Yields an Uncertain Sound*; BEC audio-tape 1969)

Apostate Christendom is unifying world religion, which under the surface is as bloodthirsty as it ever was. Once religions of the world combine with the New Age to form one great ecumenical and multi-faith monopoly, God's 'little flock' will yet again be as lambs to the slaughter.

'Wake up' is the cry of the watchman. Regardless of the cost, our responsibility is to speak out the truth to all whom we might reach, and redouble our prayers that Christ's words in Matthew 7:22 will not apply to them.

> *Many will say to me in that day, Lord, Lord, have we not prophesied in Thy name? and in Thy name have cast out devils? and in Thy name done many wonderful works? And then will I profess unto them, I never knew you: depart from me, ye that work iniquity.*

Bibliography

The Holy Bible, Authorised King James Version

d'Aubigne, Merle, *The Reformation in England*, (2 vols) Banner of Truth

lo Bello, Nino, *The Vatican Papers*, 1982

Boettner, Lorraine, *Roman Catholicism*, Banner of Truth, 1962

Chapman, Isabel, *Come Out of Her My People*, ICM, Ulveston, Cumbria LA12 8HR

Charnock, Stephen, *The New Birth*, Banner of Truth (544pp)

Chiniquy, Charles, *50 Years in the Church of Rome*, Penfold BBH, Oxon

Close, Albert, *Jesuit Plots*, Protestant Truth Society, London EC4A 2HJ
Rome's Fight for the British Throne, PTS, 184 Fleet Street, London EC4

Chick, Jack T., *Smokescreens*, Penfold BBH, PO Box 26, Bicester OX6 8PB

Compton, Piers, *The Broken Cross*

Davies, Eryl, *Truth Under Attack*, 1990, Evangelical Press, Darlington

Dickens, A.G., *The English Reformation*, 1964, Fontana/Collins

Foxe, John, *Acts and Monuments*, Seeley and Burnside, London, 1837
Foxe's Book of Martyrs, Zondervan, Grand Rapids, Michigan

Guinness, H. Grattan, *Romanism and the Reformation*, Focus Christian Ministries

Harris, Thomas, *Rome's Responsibility for the Assassination of Lincoln*, Pilgrim Brethren Press, Petersberg, Ohio

Hebblethwaite, Peter, *In the Vatican*, 1987

Hislop, Alexander, *The Two Babylons*

Hume, Cardinal Basil, *Towards a Civilization of Love*

Hunt, Dave, *Global Peace and the Rise of the Antichrist*, Harvest House, Eugene, OR 97402

Hunt, Dave, *The Berean Call* (bulletin), PO Box 7019, Bend, OR, USA

Jackson, Bill, *The Noble Army of Heretics*, CEC, PO Box 2, Liverpool

Jones, R. Tudor, *The Great Reformation*, 1985, Inter-Varsity Press

Kimball, William, *The Bible and Roman Catholicism*, Christian Equippers International PO Box 16100, S. Lake Tahoe, CA 95706

Knight, Stephen, *The Brotherhood*

Ladenius, Fred, *Amazing John XXIII*, Gift Publications, Costa Mesa, CA

Lawrence, John, *Freemasonry – a Religion?*, 1987, Kingsway Publications

Lehmann, J.H., *Behind the Dictators*, 1942, Agrora Publishing Co., NY

Lloyd-Jones, Martyn, *Knowing the Times*, Banner of Truth (400pp)

Livesey, Roy, *Understanding the New Age*, 1990, New Wine Press

Manhattan, Avro, *Vatican Imperialism in the 20th Century*, Zondervan
The Dollar and the Vatican, 1988; *Vatican Billions*, 1983; *The Vatican's Holocaust*, 1986, Ozark Books, Springfield, MO

Martin, Malachi, *The Keys of This Blood*, 1990, Simon & Schuster, NY

Martindale, CC, S.J., *What Happened at Fatima*, Catholic Truth Society

Masters, Peter and Whitcomb, John, *The Charismatic Phenomenon*, 1988

McConnell, D.R., *A Different Gospel*, 1988, Hendrikson Publishers

Molland W.H., *Salvation, the Gift of God or the Choice of Man,* 1986

Murray, Iain, *The Puritan Hope; The Fight of Faith – 1939–1981,* (biography of D. Martyn Lloyd-Jones), Banner of Truth

Nicolini, A., *History of the Jesuits,* 1987

Paris, Edmond, *The Vatican Contre La France,* 1957; *Convert or Die; The Secret History of the Jesuits; The Vatican Against Europe; Genocide in Satellite Croatia*

Puhl, Louis J., S.J., *The Spiritual Exercises of St. Ignatius,* 1951

Ranaghan, Kevin, *Catholic Pentecostalism,* 1969

Ridley, Jasper, *The Statesman and the Fanatic,* 1982, Constable, London

Robertson, Pat, *The Secret Kingdom,* 1982

de Rosa, Peter, *Vicars of Christ, the Dark Side of the Papacy,* 1988

Shepherd, J.E.C., *The Babington Plot,* Wittenburg Publications, Toronto

Short, Martin, *Inside the Brotherhood,* 1989, Guild Publications, London

Suenens, Cardinal Leon, *A New Pentecost,* 1975

Thomas, G. & Morgan-Witts, M., *Pontiff,* 1983

Walsh, Walter, *The Secret History of the Oxford Movement,* 1899

Woodrow, Ralph, *Babylon Mystery Religion,* Riverside Publications, CA

Wylie, J.A., *The History of Protestantism* (3 vols), Cassell, 1874–7

Yallop, David, *In God's Name,* Corgi Books, PO Box 11, Falmouth, Cornwall

Spirit of '88 Book List

Edwards, Brian, *God's Outlaw,* (William Tyndale) 180pp: £5.00

Gardner, David, *Sound the Trumpet Among the Nations,* 253pp: £5.00

Jackson, Bill, *The Final Flock,* 156pp: £4.50

Mitchell, E. & J., *The Two Headed Dragon of Africa,* 480pp: £7.50

Moshay, G.J.O., *Who is this Allah*, 176pp (Nigerian Edition): £4.00

Reisinger, E.C., *The Carnal Christian*, 24pp: £1.00

Ryle, J.C., *Five English Reformers*, 156pp: £3.00

Samuel, Leith, *Time to Wake Up*, 158pp: £5.50

Wilcox, J.C., *Contending for the Faith*, 156pp: £2.00

Spirit of '88 Booklets

All's Well or Sound the Alarm?, 48pp: £1.00

Maastrict, Monarchy and Morality, 8pp: *50p*, 10–£3.00, 100–£15.00

Was the Reformation a Mistake?, 8pp: *50p*, 10–£3.00, 100–£15.00

Will We Remember Them?, 8pp: *50p*, 10–£3.00, 100–£15.00

Why Were the Reformers Burned?, 8pp: *50p*, 10–£3.00, 100–£15.00

1988 Christian Heritage brochure, (A4): *40p*, 10–£2.50

The Message of Brighton '91, 8pp: *25p*, 10–£1.00

Other Booklets

Bennett, Richard, *From Tradition to Truth*, *25p*, 20–£2.00, 100–£5.50

Bennett, Richard, *The Bible vs Roman Catholicism*, *25p*, 20–£2.00, 100–£5.50

Mawhinney, Stanley, *Evangelical Catholics: a New Phenomenon*, 36pp: £2.00

Samuel, David, *The End of the Ecumenical Movement*, 20pp: £1.00

Wordsworth, Christopher, *Is the Papacy Predicted by St. Paul?*: £1.00

Lee, Francis N., *Antichrist in Scripture*, 58pp: £3.00

(Postage to be added to these prices for overseas orders)

Spirit of '88: Dorchester House, Marsham Lane, Gerrards Cross, Bucks, England, WD3 5PW
Registered Charity No: 327574

Index

People

Organisations, Publications, Events